Fifty Easy
Old-Fashioned
Flowers

Fifty Easy Old-Fashioned Flowers

Anne M. Zeman

Henry Holt and Company
New York

Henry Holt and Company, Inc.
Publishers since 1866
115 West 18th Street
New York, New York 10011

Library of Congress Cataloging-in-Publication Data
Zeman, Anne M.
Fifty easy old-fashioned flowers / Anne M. Zeman. — 1st ed.
p.   cm.
"An Irving Place Press book" — T.p. verso
Includes index.
1. Flowers—Heirloom varieties. 2. Flower gardening.
I. Title.
SB407.Z45 1995   95-9095
635.9—dc20   CIP
ISBN 0-8050-3978-3

Henry Holt books are available for special promotions and premiums.
For details contact: Director, Special Markets.

First Edition—1995

AN IRVING PRESS PLACE BOOK
Designed by Charlotte Staub

Printed in Hong Kong
All first editions are printed on acid-free paper. ∞

1 3 5 7 9 10 8 6 4 2

For Mark

ACKNOWLEDGMENTS

Gardening is a shared experience: the sharing of knowledge, plants, and time. Many people were kind enough to share these things with me as I researched, wrote, and gathered photographs for this book:

Michelle Haynes, lifelong friend and fellow gardener, who always has time to discuss the merits and difficulties of plants, and who traveled with me to many of the gardens and nurseries where we studied and photographed flowers for this book.

Charles Cresson, an extraordinary plantsman, who was kind enough to review the manuscript and suggest ways to make the book better.

Kate Kelly, my friend and partner, whose editorial and professional skills are without equal.

Many thanks, too, to Ray Roberts for his enthusiastic support and guidance, to Ben Ratliff for his attention to detail, and to Charlotte Staub for creating a beautiful book design.

My family was very supportive during writing of this book, particularly my husband, Mark, who constantly encourages me to install new gardens to reduce his lawnmowing time. And gratitude must also be expressed to my faithful feline companion, Libby, who slept in my lap through much of the writing this book.

I would also like to thank the following people who generously shared their photography: Liz Ball, Kathy Wilkinson Barash, Charles Cresson, Michelle Haynes, Mike Lowe, Jack Potter, and Mike Shoup.

Contents

Introduction

Over the past several years, old-fashioned flowers have enjoyed a renaissance. Nurseries and major catalog companies who, ten years ago, stocked only the newest hybrids, now offer a multitude of these classic beauties. Often called "heirloom" flowers, many of the old-fashioned flowers are re-introductions of plants once popular from the turn of the century and earlier. Easy to grow, less susceptible to pests or diseases, old-fashioned flowers have been deservedly rediscovered, and the demand for them grows each year.

Perhaps the interest in old-fashioned flowers stems from memories of the flowers our mothers and grandmothers grew. The sweet perfume of pinks nestled by the back door, brighty-colored cosmos sneaking through the backyard fence, or hedges of giant hollyhocks towering against the shed evoke thoughts of simpler times—of childhood, or family, or days when the pace of life was slower and gentler.

Another reason for the renewed interest is fragrance. The perfume of old-fashioned flowers is deeper and richer than that of their modern cousins. In many new varieties, scent has been sacrificed al-together for form. Another advantage of old-fashioneds is their hardiness and easiness. Some plants, such as peonies, thrive for years on neglect. Others, if left undisturbed, return year after year from abundant self-sowing. Many of the old classics are also little bothered by pests, including insects, mildews, and rusts.

"Old-fashioned" means many things. For furniture, old-fashioned usually means antiques some seventy-five or more years old. For cars, classic comes at thirty years of age. In clothing, old-fashioned means last year's wardrobe. In horticulture, roses are old-fashioned if they were bred before the first Hybrid Tea in 1867. But for flowers, there is no hard and fast rule. Old-fashioned may simply mean familiar flowers grown in the garden during childhood summers. For this book, old-fashioned means flowers that have been in cultivation for approximately 100 years. Many are significantly older. Some of our best known garden flowers have existed for over two thousand years, among them peonies, hollyhocks, daffodils, lilies, marigolds, and foxgloves.

Readers of other garden books will often find the term "old-fashioned" used interchangeably with "English cottage garden." Of course, no book on old-fashioned flowers would be complete without mentioning English primroses or hollyhocks; but, unlike other books, the flowers discussed here include many North American species. The gardens of Montezuma were a horticultural wonder in the 1500s. Among the flowers in the highly developed Aztec gardens were such cherished old-fashioned favorites as zinnias, dahlias, sunflowers, and morning glories.

Native Americans and the early settlers also played an important role in determining the flowers favored from generation to generation of family gardeners. European colonists brought with them a love of flowers from the Old World. Among their personal belongings were tucked favorite seeds and cuttings of a beloved plant, a living symbol of hope and promise for growth and prosperity in a new land. In addition to importing plants from Europe, settlers also adopted for their gardens the native plants that they found useful. The Native Americans shared plants and showed them medicinal and other uses for the indiginous flora. These native flowers—among them sunflowers, evening primroses, bee balms, and California poppies—became fast favorites of all North American cultures.

In *Fifty Easy Old-Fashioned Flowers,* plants are arranged in alphabetical order by common name for ease of reference. Genus and species names follow each main heading. Each has been chosen for its ease of cultivation, hardiness, and beauty, as well as for its age. Each variety is available to the modern gardener and each provides a tradition and charm to brighten any garden. Histories and concise descriptions of the fifty flowers are provided in the text, including growing instructions and tips for cultivating these classic beauties.

Some wonderful old-fashioned flowers are not included because they are too challenging to grow. For example, delphiniums are very sensitive to soil and climate conditions. Lupines grow easily in the Northeast and Pacific Northwest, but elsewhere fare poorly, and so were omitted from the core fifty.

—Anne M. Zeman

*Fifty Easy
Old-Fashioned
Flowers*

Aster

New York Aster, *Aster novi-belgii*
New England Aster, *Aster novae angliae*

FOLKLORE

The aster has delighted generations at least as far back as Virgil, who, in mellifluous verse, described its beauty and recounted how aster wreaths were used by the gods and goddesses on temple altars. Perhaps antedating Virgil's poetry is the ancient Greek legend of Virgo weeping. As he gazed down from heaven, his tears mixed with stardust and asters were created. The name *Aster* is the same as the Greek word meaning "star," and refers to the flower's star-like appearance. The ancient Greeks are also said to have used asters to drive away snakes and as an antidote for snake bites and poisons.

In the late 1600s, asters were mixed into ointments thought to cure the bite of mad dogs. The Shakers used the plant to clear their complexions. In Germany, the aster is plucked petal by petal to decide if a love is returned or not.

The New York aster was identified by the Belgian botanist Hermann in 1786 and named after the area of origin, New Amsterdam. The English call these asters Michaelmas daisies (Michaelmas Day is September 29).

DESCRIPTION

One of the most spectacular perennials in the garden from late August until November, asters have a many-petaled, daisy-like flower that comes in pink, pale blue, purple, or white, all growing from a yellow central disk. Reaching heights from 4 to 6 feet with dark green, lance-shaped leaves, these hardy perennials offer massive numbers of large, clustered blooms on branching stems. Asters are excellent for forming bold masses of color in the garden and they are good for cutting.

CULTIVATION

An easy plant to grow, asters adapt to any kind of soil with good drainage, but will be more vigorous when grown in rich soil and fertilized regularly in the spring. It's best to put out newly purchased or divided plants in the spring or early summer. Seeds planted in the spring will bloom the following year.

Pinch the tips early in the season for bushier plants. Water regularly. Old-fashioned asters usually need staking, which should be done in the spring before they fall and continued as they grow. Divide the plants every three or four years.

COMMENTS: There are numerous hybrids available in various heights and spreads. For the hot, humid summers of the South, try the long-blooming *Aster* x *frikartii*. The old-fashioned annual asters are called China asters and are botanically known as *Callistephus*.

POSITION: Sun or part shade.

PROPAGATION: Seed, division, or cuttings.

New England aster (above). *Aster* x *frikartii* (opposite)

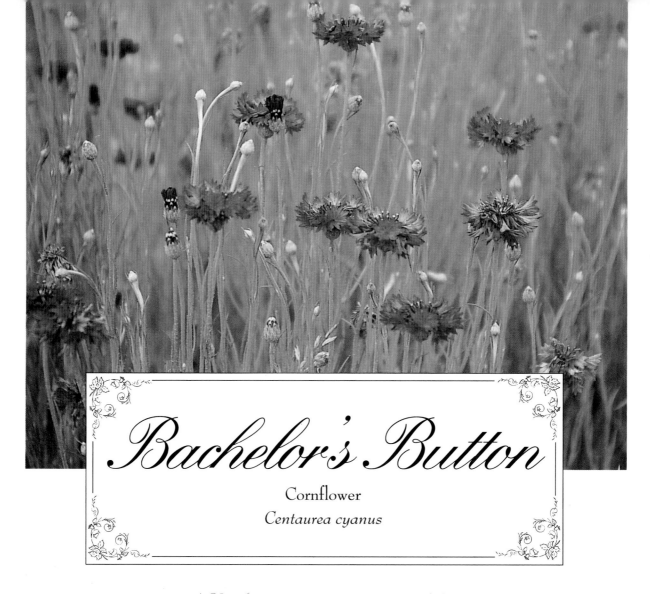

Bachelor's Button

Cornflower

Centaurea cyanus

❧ FOLKLORE ❧

The genus name *Centaurea* is taken from the myth of the Greek centaurs, who were half man and half horse. The centaur Chiron—known for his wisdom in medicine and prophecy, as well as his skills in the arts and hunting—was shot in the foot by a poison arrow from Hercules's bow. Chiron administered cornflower to his wound, and he was healed. In mythology, Chiron is credited for having taught mankind the use of medicinal plants, although we now know that cornflowers have no great medicinal value.

Cornflowers were among the jewelry and gold discovered in the tomb of King Tutankhamen. A small wreath of cornflowers and olive leaves, still the deepest blue after thousands of years, was among the cache of riches left to aid the pharaoh in the afterlife.

Cornflowers were brought to America from Europe in the seventeenth century and were among the flowers cultivated by Thomas Jefferson at Monticello. Often called the "cultivated weed" or "weed of the cornfield," cornflower got its name because it was the flowering weed that grew among the corn plants. The moniker bachelor's button became popular when men began wearing cornflowers as boutonnieres.

DESCRIPTION

Prized for their intense blue color, cornflowers have been featured in gardens for more than a hundred years. Most varieties are blue, but others come in pink, maroon, and white blooms, set apart by pale, gray-green leaves. Bachelor's buttons grow 1 to 3 feet and bloom in early summer. Leave some seedheads after these annuals flower and goldfinches will visit your garden to eat the seeds. Bachelor's buttons last for up to two weeks as a cut flower and they are also nice dried.

CULTIVATION

Bachelor's buttons grow in almost any soil. They can withstand mild frosts but do not transplant well. Sow seeds directly in the garden in early spring as soon as the soil can be worked; start seeds indoors about 4 weeks before setting out. Thin seedlings to 8 to 10 inches apart. Make successive plantings every two weeks to extend bloom time in the garden. Water only moderately, being careful not to overwater, to help prevent disease. Cut faded blooms to prolong flowering. Sun and cool temperatures produce the best results. In warmer climates, seeds can be sown in autumn. Bachelor's buttons often self-seed.

COMMENTS: *C. montana*, commonly called mountain bluet, is a perennial similar to the annual bachelor's button. It produces masses of blooms up to 18 inches high in late spring and early summer.

POSITION: Sun.

PROPAGATION: Seed for annuals; seed, division, or cuttings for perennials.

Balsam

Touch-Me-Not, Lady Slipper

Impatiens balsamina

FOLKLORE

Balsam, native to tropical Asia, is believed to have been introduced to Europe about 1540, where it was first grown as a single flower. It was a popular summer bedding plant among gardeners of early Tudor England. In the early 1800s, the first camellia-flowered types were developed and the popularity of balsam soared to make it a particular favorite in Victorian gardens.

Both the genus and the common name *Impatiens* refer to a characteristic of the seed capsule. When the ripe pods are touched, they burst suddenly and seeds scatter, as if impatient. The impatient burst of seeds also inspired the name Touch-Me-Not.

Double balsam, a two-flowered variety, was planted at Shadwell, Thomas Jefferson's boyhood home, as early as 1767, and later at Monticello. The plants were started in hot beds (cold frames heated by decomposing manure).

Balsam plants have long been used to make dye. In India, the dyes are favored for fabrics. Silks and wools of yellow and red traditionally have been created with balsam dyes. In Japan, a red dye extracted from balsam was used as a paint for finger nails.

Balsam is also used as a curative. To this day, herbalists apply balsam to insect bites and use it to relieve the itch of poison ivy.

DESCRIPTION

An old-time favorite, balsam has been culti-vated for generations. A distinct and unusual plant, it looks quite different for the impatiens so widely grown today.

Pyramid-shaped plants, 12 to 36 inches high, produce a single main stem bearing brilliant double flowers shaped like small camellias. The double flowers grow along the stalk and come in white, pink, red, purple, and yellow, some spotted or striped. The leaves are a medium green, about 6 inches long, and pointed. At one time a very popu-lar garden annual, balsam lostfavor over the years but is now being revived be gardeners in new forms and hybrids.

CULTIVATION

Annual balsams are easy and satisfying to grow. The plants are free-flowering, resistant to heat and heavy rain, and adaptable to sun or shade. They do well in hot summers. Balsams do not require re-moval of spent blooms, and they will naturalize eas-ily, reappearing the following year from self-sown seeds. Balsams can also be transplanted in full bloom. Sow balsam seeds outdoors in place or start them indoors 6 to 8 weeks before the last frost. Cover the seeds lightly—light is needed to germi-nate—and keep the soil warm. Plant in light, sandy soil, somewhat rich and moist, and space 10 to 18 inches apart, fertilizing and watering regularly. Some of the taller balsam specimens benefit from topping, or pinching back, the leaves to make bushier plants.

COMMENT: Balsam does not do as well in full shade as *Impatiens wallerana*, the impatiens so abundant at today's nurseries.

POSITION: Sun or light shade.

Balsam 'African Queen' (above). Pink and rose balsam (opposite).

Bee Balm

Scarlet Bergamot, Oswego Tea
Monarda didyma

❧ FOLKLORE ❧

Native to eastern North America, bee balm is also known as Indian plume, fragrant balm, and mountain mint. Another name developed when the residents of Oswego, New York, on Lake Ontario, used bee balm leaves to make a tea. The tea became popular, especially during the Revolutionary War, in the neighboring New England states, where it was dubbed Oswego Tea. Documents of the late eighteenth century recommended planting bee balm plentifully in the kitchen garden for the purpose of brewing Oswego Tea.

During the 1700s on a plant-collecting trip around the country, the American botanist John Bartram collected seeds from Oswego and sent them to England. The tea seems to have been less popular among Britons, where the bright scarlet flowers of bee balm became more a feature of the decorative border than the kitchen garden.

A member of the mint family, bee balm has a strong flavor that is desirable as seasoning in cooking. Bee balm was also traditionally used to soothe stomachaches and sore throats, and to reduce fevers.

The genus name *Monarda* was chosen for Dr. Nicholas Monardes, a Spanish physician, who published an important book on plants of the New World.

The species name, *didyma*, is from a Greek word meaning "paired," and refers to the twin stamens in each flower.

DESCRIPTION

Bee balm is among the few plants that possess not only fragrant leaves, but also brilliant flowers. The small tubular flowers, arranged in whorls, form a dense cluster, 2 to 3 inches wide. Blooms are mostly red, but also come in pink, white, or purple. Bee balm blooms from late June into August. Bee balm's red flowers and the tubular arrangement of the blossoms attract hummingbirds, bees, and butterflies. The foliage forms dense clumps of erect, square stems, 2 to 3 feet tall. Bee balm leaves, like other members of the mint family, are aromatic when crushed. Bee balm is particularly effective when massed in loose clumps or in other informal arrangements.

CULTIVATION

Hardy bee balm plants thrive in any ordinary soil, provided it is cool and moist. Plant in full sun or part shade; part shade is best for longer-lasting flowers. Bee balm is not drought tolerant, so soil should be kept moist; without moisture, the plants become susceptible to powdery mildew and rust. Bee balm is vigorous and can spread rapidly. Withhold fertilizer to slow rapid spreading. Divide the plants in spring every three to four years to avoid tall, lanky growth. Sow seeds outdoors in spring or fall for bloom the following season. Purchased plants should be spaced 18 to 24 inches apart.

Bee balm is readily propagated by its creeping roots.

COMMENTS: *Monarda fistulosa*, known as wild bergamot, grows in dry soil as well as moist, making it a better choice for drier climates.

POSITION: Sun or part shade.

Bleeding Heart

Lady's Locket, *Dicentra spectabilis*

FOLKLORE

The name bleeding heart aptly describes the little rosy-red, heart-shaped flowers with their extension that looks like a drop of blood. Other common names for this plant are lady's locket, lyre flower, and lady-in-the-bath.

The bleeding heart was imported from the Orient to Europe by the Jesuit missionary d'Incarville around the middle of the eighteenth century, but it was not cultivated until 1847, when Robert Fortune, an English botanist, found it on the Japanese Isle of Chusan and sent it back to England.

Within a very short time, bleeding heart could be found in virtually every Victorian garden.

Bleeding heart was also popular among nineteenth-century gardeners in the eastern United States. But as pioneers moved West, bleeding heart seeds grew harder to come by, and the native fringed bleeding heart (*D. exima*) and Pacific bleeding heart (*D. formosa*) became attractive substitutes.

The genus name *Dicentra* comes from the Greek words *dis* (twice) and *kentron* (spur), and means "doubled spurred." *Spectabilis* means "remarkable."

DESCRIPTION

Bleeding hearts are graceful plants with long racemes of drooping, heart-shaped flowers in either reddish-pink or white. The elegant foliage is green with a slightly gray cast and deeply cut leaves. The plant forms dense clumps up to 2 feet wide, and from 2 to 3 feet high. The brightly colored blooms appear in early April and last until the end of June.

An excellent plant for the shade, bleeding heart blooms even in full shade, although sparingly. The foliage dies down in summer. To mask the spent foliage, plant annuals or perennials, such as hosta or ferns, over it.

CULTIVATION

Plant in warm, light, rich, well-drained soil in partial shade. Bleeding heart will do nicely in full sun, but the leaves tend to fade. Place plants 1½ to 2 feet apart. Water regularly and fertilize in early spring. Propagate by division in early spring. Starting bleeding heart by seed is moderately difficult, and requires both work and patience. Seeds can be started indoors in flats, but must be refrigerated for 5 to 6 weeks before germination. Seeds can also be sown outdoors in late fall or early winter; keep the soil moist until the ground freezes. For greatest ease, purchase plants in early spring.

COMMENTS: *D. exima*, the fringed bleeding heart, and *D. formosa*, Pacific bleeding heart, are native to North America and are much smaller plants than *D. spectabilis*. Fringed bleeding heart grows from 12 to 18 inches. Although not quite as brilliant in color as common bleeding heart, it is hardier, blooms off and on all summer, and readily self-sows. It also comes in pink and white.

POSITION: Part shade or shade.

Common bleeding heart, *Dicentra spectabilis* (above). Fringed bleeding heart, *D. exima* (opposite).

Calendula

Pot Marigold, *Calendula officinalis*

Dedicated to the Virgin Mary and known as Mary's gold, calendula is described by Shakespeare in *The Winter's Tale* as the "winking Mary-buds" of Cymbeline. The Elizabethans cultivated the pot marigold almost exclusively for medicinal applications. Among the ills calendula purportedly soothed were smallpox, measles, fevers, and the sting of a wasp or a bee. An ointment made with calendula was used to dress cuts, burns, and sores. During the U.S. Civil War, surgeons used calendula to treat wounds. It's often recounted that Gertrude Jekyll, the famous English gardener, grew an abundance of calendula during World War I and sent it to first aid stations for treatment of injuries. Calendula has also been used in cooking as a seasoning for broths, wine, and salads, and the calendula petals were often substituted for saffron.

The genus name is from the Latin *calund*, which refers to the first part of the month. In Roman times, calendula could be found in bloom in almost every month of the year.

14

DESCRIPTION

Despite its common name and appearance, calendula is not a true marigold at all. It belongs to the same family, but is of a different genus. Unlike true marigolds, calendula leaves are undivided and do not have the distinct odor of today's marigold (*Tagestes*).

Calendula are hardy garden annuals. They are easy to grow, and they produce a vivid display of color over a long growing season. The flower heads are 3 to 4 inches across and come in lemon, gold, orange, and cream in single, daidy-like flowers, or in double, chrysanthemum-like flowers. The foliage is dark green. Calendual's long stems grow 10 to 24 inches, making trhem ideal for cutting. Generously blooming from July to frost, calendula are excellent for containers and planters.

CULTIVATION

Hardy enough to withstand several frosts, calendula seeds may be sown outdoors as soon as the soil can be worked. Seeds can be started indoors 4 to 6 weeks before the last frost, but take care not to disturb the long taproots when transplanting. Move seedlings or purchased plants to the garden two weeks before the last frost, spacing 10 to 15 inches apart. Calendula adapts to most any soil, but thrives in light, sandy, and moderately rich ones.

Fertilize when planting and keep the faded flowers picked off for continuous bloom. Calendula performs best in temperatures under 85°F, but can be used as a spring or fall plant in hot climates. Make a second planting in July or August for fall color and winter blooms. In mild climates, blooms can last all winter long. Calendula self-sows readily, although doubles sometimes revert back to the single-bloom parent.

POSITION: Sun or light shade.

PROPAGATION: Seed.

Candytuft

Iberis umbellata

FOLKLORE

Candytuft is not named for a sweet, as the name might suggest, but rather drew its moniker from its place of origin, Candia, the ancient name of Crete. First found growing on the shores of the Mediterranean, the plant has been cultivated since 1596, and has ever since been a familiar plant in cottage gardens.

In Elizabethan England, candytuft seeds were used to make mustard for meat. Candytuft was also thought to aid indigestion, and was used to treat rheumatism and gout. Candytuft mixtures were also made to treat asthma and bronchitis. In fact, candytuft was favored as a medicinal, rather than an ornamental plant.

The genus name *Iberis*—derived from Iberia, the ancient name for Spain, where several species of candytuft grow wild—inspired candytuft's alternate name, Spanish tufts. The English called it sciatic cress and Billy-come-home-soon.

DESCRIPTION

A lovely border plant with globe-shaped flower heads formed by clusters of small, four-petaled flowers, candytuft comes in all shades of pink, rose, white, and lavender. The leaves are 2 to 3 inches long and form a tidy mound, 10 to 15 inches tall.

Candytuft blooms in early summer in a dense mass of flowers, and blooms again in early fall. Plants will bloom longer if spent blooms are removed.

This annual plant is excellent for city gardens as well as country gardens, as it is not sensitive to air quality.

CULTIVATION

Candytuft tolerates long periods of drought and almost any kind of soil condition, but it cannot live in shade or thrive in excessive moisture. Sow seeds outdoors after the last frost, or start indoors 6 to 8 weeks ahead. In frost-free areas, sow seeds in the late fall for June flowers.

To extend the flowering season, sow at 2-week intervals for several weeks in spring. Thin to 6 or 8 inches apart and fertilize when planting. Deadhead regularly for more blooms. Cut plants back if they become tall and floppy. This will result in new growth and additional blooms.

COMMENTS: *I. amara*, rocket candytuft, bears large, cone-shaped flowers that have a sweet, fresh fragrance.

POSITION: Sun.

PROPAGATION: Seed or cuttings.

Canna

Canna Lily, Indian Shot
Canna species

FOLKLORE

Native to South and Central America and the West Indies, cannas were first offered for sale in Europe at the Stockholm flower markets in 1880. By 1906, these brilliant flowers had became the rage throughout Europe, with over 1,100 varieties on the market. Cannas were also very popular in the United States until the 1950s, when other varieties became more fashionable.

Canna is sometimes called Indian shot because its hard, round seeds resemble shot gun pellets. Native South Americans used canna seeds to make jewelry, especially necklaces. Spanish explorers brought a number of these seeds back to Spain during the sixteenth century, where the large seeds were used as rosary beads.

The name *Canna* comes from the Latin meaning "reed" or "cane," and refers to the appearance of the flower stalk.

DESCRIPTION

Cannas are one of the most exotic looking plants in the garden. Large, vividly colored, with beautiful foliage, they are spectacular when massed or placed in the back of a border. These dramatic plants are easy to cultivate, fast-growing, and very long-flowering, blooming all season to first frost.

The showy flowers come in a wide range of colors, from yellow and orange, to red, pink, and salmon, to cream. The unusually large leaves range from green to bronze or brown, or are variegated. The numerous varieties now available vary in height from 3 to 7 feet. Dwarf varieties can be grown in pots.

CULTIVATION

Cannas thrive in long, hot summers and flourish in rich, organic soil, but perform adequately in poor soil, provided they have ample moisture. Plant rhizomes 1 inch deep and 18 inches apart directly in the garden in warm soil after the last frost. Water regularly. Cannas can survive dry periods, but

blooms will suffer. Remove dead blooms continuously. In late summer or fall, cut back the stems to just above soil level and mulch heavily. Rhizomes may be left in the ground where the soil doesn't freeze; otherwise, they should be lifted and stored over winter.

COMMENTS: The wild species, *C. flaccida*, is native to South Carolina and Florida, and is one of the principal parents of the modern species.

POSITION: Sun.

PROPAGATION: Division or seed.

Canna 'Pretoria' (left). *Canna* 'Polly Gay' (right). *Canna* 'The President' (opposite).

Canterbury Bells

Bellflower, Cup and Saucer
Campanula medium

FOLKLORE

Beautiful and beloved, Canterbury bells are said to resemble the bells the pilgrims used to decorate their horses as they journeyed to the shrine of Thomas à Becket at Canterbury Cathedral in England. The English also call these flowers Coventry bells because they are found growing among the hedgerows in Coventry.

Cultivated since 1597, Canterbury bells were grown by the sixteenth century horticulturist John Gerard, who wrote about them in his *Herball of Plants.*

A plant often associated with early American flower gardens, Canterbury bells were offered for sale on this continent as seed as early as 1760. They were among the flowers grown by George Washington at Mount Vernon. Thomas Jefferson planted them along the avenue leading to his beloved Monticello.

DESCRIPTION

Massed together in groups, Canterbury bells make a stunning statement in the old-fashioned and modern garden alike.

Biennials grown as annuals, these plants bear spikes of purple, lavender, pink, and white bell-shaped flowers. The flowers are 1 inch or more in diameter and grow abundantly in loose, open clusters on stems reaching 24 to 36 inches high. Blooms last from June to early August.

Canterbury bells have the largest flower of all the campanulas. The cup and saucer is a semi-double type, and dwarf plants are available with smaller, daintier bellflowers. Campanulas make long-lasting cut flowers.

CULTIVATION

Although some perennial forms of campanulas take 2 or 3 years to mature, Canterbury bells are easy to grow from seed, even easier if seedlings are purchased at the nursery, and offer satisfying results the same season. Start seeds indoors 8 to 10 weeks ahead for flowers the first year. The very fine seed should not be covered—light is essential for germination.

Traditionally, Canterbury bells are sown in July or August for flowering the following summer. Plant in rich, moist, but well-drained soil, and space or thin seedlings 10 to 12 inches apart. Fertilize monthly and water regularly, keeping soil moist. Snip off faded flower spikes. Canterbury bells may reseed themselves. Taller varieties will topple over unless they are staked.

COMMENTS: All species of *Campanula* are referred to by the common name of bellflower. Most are perennials, and blooms come in a great variety of blues and purples. The peach-leaf bellflower (*C. persicifolia*) is one of the easiest to grow and most attractive.

POSITION: Sun or light shade.

PROPAGATION: Seed.

Celosia

Cockscomb, *Celosia argentea*, var. *cristata*,
Cristata Group; Plume Celosia, *C. argentea*,
var. *cristata*, Plumosa Group

FOLKLORE

A popular plant in colonial America, cockscomb was grown at Mount Vernon by George Washington and at Monticello by Thomas Jefferson, who noted in his journals in 1767 that it was a "handsome plant" but quite a "curiosity." Popular throughout America, cockscomb was especially favored in the early 1900s, when it was regularly exhibited in pots at small fairs, where the smallest plants producing the largest crests took the prizes.

Native to the Asiatic tropics, cockscomb was cultivated in Britain in 1597, where it became quite the rage to grow indoors or in a greenhouse, presumably because it was thought too tender for cultivation outdoors. Because of this, Elizabethans often called it floramor or flower gentle. The name cockscomb was given to the plant because it resembles a rooster's comb.

The genus name *Celosia* comes from the Greek word *kelos*, meaning "burned," and refers to the plant's brilliant red and orange flame-like colors. Because of its lasting blooms, both in the garden and in pots indoors, the plant has come to symbolize longevity.

DESCRIPTION

Cockscomb is an unusual, exotic-looking plant that blooms from June to frost. The flower heads are fan-like clumps that resemble a rooster's comb or a clump of coral. These velvety crimson heads are striking, but are somewhat difficult to match with other plants. Use them as an accent plant away from other reds, plant them by themselves, or mass them in the front of the border.

Cockscomb's· broad flower clusters are 3 to 6 inches wide. Color ranges from crimson to orange to pink. These annuals grow 6 to 30 inches high, with medium green leaves, some variegated. Cockscomb makes a striking cut flower, and it holds color well when dried.

Plume celosia has a vertical display of feathery-looking, upright flowers that come in red, yellow, orange, pink, and purple. Sometimes likened to a flame, it grows 10 to 36 inches high. When massed together as a bedding plant, plume celosia makes a bright display.

CULTIVATION

Celosias do not transplant well, so sow outdoors in place as soon as the soil warms. To start indoors, grow seedlings in peat pots and transfer entire pots to the garden to minimize transplant shock 4 weeks prior to the last frost. Light is essential for germination, so barely cover seeds and keep them moist. Do not set out seedlings too early—make sure temperatures are above 60°F at night. Otherwise, plants will suffer permanent stunting. Place 6 to 12 inches apart and water moderately. Prepare rich, well-drained soil and fertilize only when planting. Celosias are quite tolerant of heat and drought. To dry, cut flowers at their peak and hang upside down.

POSITION: Sun or part shade.

PROPAGATION: Seed.

Yellow Plume celosia (left). Cockscomb (right). Red Plume celosia (opposite).

Columbine

Aquilegia canadensis, Aquilegia vulgaris

Since the Middle Ages, columbine has graced gardens. Its praises have been sung in literature as early as 1310 and later in the works of Chaucer, Skelton, and Shakespeare. Artists, too, have been enamored of its beauty; its blossoms have appeared in paintings for centuries.

Columbine was once an essential ingredient in medical remedies. Used to cure the measles, small pox, and liver ailments, it was also thought to remedy jaundice, especially if taken with saffron. Columbine is one of the eight herbs cited in 1373 by an anonymous author of a treatment for plague. People ceased using columbine in remedies in the mid-eighteenth century, however, when Swedish botanist Carolus Linnaeus warned that children could die from an overdose.

By the seventeenth century, columbine had become a symbol of cuckoldry, and bouquets of these flowers were presented only to those women who were thought to possess loose morals. The Victorians later associated the flowers with folly and thanklessness.

DESCRIPTION

Columbine is a graceful perennial with long, swinging spurs that extend from the blossom. The North american native *Aquilegia canadensis* has cheerful red and yellow blooms, and *A. vulgaris*, European columbine, blooms in shades of blue, pink, white, and purple. Once established, columbine blooms freely and self-sows. The fancier hybrids, in blue lavender, yellow, red, pink, white, and bi-color, are not as easy to grow as the two old-fashioned favorites. Columbine has elegant, fern-like foliage of blue-green that remains attractive after the blooms have faded. Plants range from 18 to 36 inches high and bloom in May and June. The spurs contain nectar that attracts hummingbirds.

CULTIVATION

Columbine grows quickly from seed when sown directly outdoors in early spring or summer for flowers the next season. Do not cover the seeds and keep the soil moist to ensure good germination. To start indoors, seeds must be refrigerated in flats for three weeks prior to germination. Columbines are not long-lived, but they're easy to raise from seed, and it is easy to keep them ongoing by successive planting. Sow in rich, light soil, about 10 inches apart and keep plants watered during dry spells. Regularly remove spent flowers to prolong bloom. For self-sowing, leave some seed heads on the plants. (If you grow hybrids, be aware that gathering your own seed to continue a plant may prove disappointing—often the plant reverts back to a parent.) Mulch for protection during winter.

COMMENTS: *A. coerulea*, Rocky Mountain columbine, is the state flower of Colorado. A beautiful, erect flower of deep blue, it is unpredictable in eastern or lowland gardens.

POSITION: Sun or part shade.

PROPAGATION: Seed.

Cosmos

Garden Cosmos, Mexican Aster

Cosmos bipinnatus

FOLKLORE

Archaeological evidence suggests that the ancient Aztecs cultivated many flowers, including cosmos. Blossoms from marigolds, crocuses, zinnias, and cosmos were ground together to make a yellow dye for clothes and other materials.

Native to Mexico, cosmos were first discovered by Spanish plant collectors who sent seeds back to Spain and later introduced the plant to Europe. First grown commercially around the 1880s, cosmos is a popular and showy member of the sunflower family native to tropical America. In the East Indies, the leaves and flowering tops of young cosmos plants are used as a potherb. When steamed, the leaves and flowers render a yellow paste used to season rice, potatoes, and other starchy foods, as well as soups, omelets, and casseroles.

The genus name *Cosmos* is from the Greek word *kosmos*, meaning "orderliness" and "perfection."

DESCRIPTION

Masses of cosmos in the summer garden are a sight to behold. These light, airy annual plants have brightly colored flowers and lacy, pale green foliage, both delicate and attractive. The wide-petaled, daisy-like flowers are 1 to 3 inches wide with a small yellow center. Among the many varieties of cosmos available, the old-fashioned, single-flowering crimson, rose, and white ones are the most popular.

Cosmos grow up to 48 inches high and bloom profusely from June to frost, sometimes lasting until November. Cosmos attract butterflies. A good cut flower, cosmos also make beautiful bouquets.

CULTIVATION

Few plants require as little care or self-sow as readily as cosmos. Purchase bedding plants or sow seed outdoors after last frost or start indoors 4 to 6 weeks ahead. Cosmos seeds are large and easy to handle. They do well in average soil and even tolerate dry and infertile soil, provided they get plenty of sun and are set in a warm spot. Rich soil will result in lavish foliage, but few, if any, flowers. Water moderately and do not fertilize. Pinch out the leading shoots of young plants to encourage bushier growth. Remove spent blooms for additional flowering. Cosmos self-sow readily and probably will not need to be replanted. Taller varieties need staking.

COMMENTS: *C. sulphureus*, yellow cosmos, was introduced in 1896. It is a shorter plant with bushier foliage than *C. bipinnatus*, and bears bright yellow, gold, or orange flowers. Plants range from a dwarf of 12 inches up to 36 inches.

POSITION: Sun or partial shade.

PROPAGATION: Seed.

Cosmos 'Sensation Mix' (above). White cosmos (opposite).

Daffodil

Narcissus species

FOLKLORE

The ancient Greeks dedicated the daffodil to Hecate, queen of the underworld, and to Demeter, Persephone's mother and goddess of fertility. The daffodil was the flower that Persephone was gathering when she was abducted by Pluto and taken to Hades.

Theophrastus mentioned the daffodil about 300 B.C. and the flower has been described in other great works of literature, including the writings of Homer, Virgil, Ovid, Sophocles, and Shakespeare. Egyptians used them in funerary wreaths, which have survived in tombs 3,000 years later. An old Welsh saying suggests that the first person lucky enough to discover the first blooming daffodil of the season will be blessed with more gold than silver.

A common belief is that the daffodil was named for the mythological character Narcissus, the self-loving youth. More than likely, the genus name was from the Greek *narkan*, meaning "narcotic," referring to the narcotic qualities of the daffodil's scent.

One of the first daffodils brought to America was "van Sion," a double of greenish-yellow color. It was once naturalized as far north as New York and can still be found in old gardens. Daffodils planted by early colonists in Virginia still bloom each spring.

DESCRIPTION

Daffodils may be the most beloved of all flowers. Their cheery yellow blooms beckon the spring. Most daffodils are yellow, but some are white, pink, and bi-colored. Some are quite fragrant. So numerous are daffodils, they have been classified into 11 divisions, ranging from small to large, trumpet to flat-petaled, and single to double. Plants range in height from 2 to 18 inches, with bloom times varying from early spring to late spring. Select different kinds of daffodils to enjoy successive blooms from February through May. Plant them informally in drifts or groups, rather than in straight lines. Daffodils are also excellent container plants and can be forced.

CULTIVATION

Daffodil culture is simple. When purchasing bulbs, buy firm ones with no soft spots or discolorations. Plant at a depth approximately twice the bulb's length in sandy loam or in most any other well-drained soil. Plant in the fall for bloom the following spring.

Daffodils are long-lived, naturalize easily, and do not need to be divided unless they produce small (or no) flowers due to overcrowding. Do not cut off the foliage—let it die naturally. The nutrients from the decomposed leaves return to the bulb; if the foliage is cut off, the bulb won't bloom or will die. Daffodils can be grown from seed, but the process is slow. It's much easier to buy bulbs.

COMMENTS: Jonquils are a distinct group of late-blooming narcissus. They have 2 to 6 fragrant, yellow flowers per stem. The terms narcissus and daffodil can be used interchangeably, but jonquils are distinct.

POSITION: Sun or part shade.

PROPAGATION: Division or seed.

Dahlia

Dahlia species

FOLKLORE

Dahlias are native to the mountainous regions of Mexico and Guatemala. At the time of the Spanish conquest of Mexico (1519-1524), dahlias were being cultivated by the Aztecs, who called the plant *cocoxochitl*, or "water pipe," a name that refers to the plant's hollow stalk.

Dahlias reached Europe around 1790, when seed was sent to Madrid from Mexico. The dahlia reached Holland in 1804 and later, France and England. The Empress Josephine grew dahlias in her famous gardens at Malmaison near Paris in the early 1800s. By the 1830s, a great dahlia craze swept Europe. The flower grew so popular that in 1826 there were 62 types cultivated in England; by 1841 there were 1,220. In 1864, the Caledonian Horticultural Society offered 50,000 francs to the person who could cultivate a blue dahlia. The prize was never claimed. There is no record of the dahlia's introduction into the United States, but many varieties were being grown here as early as 1821.

The dahlia is named for Andreas Dahl, a Swedish botanist and pupil of Carolus Linnaeus.

DESCRIPTION

Most of the dahlias available today are compact, low-growing hybrids. They bloom from early summer to frost, and come in a multitude of shapes, sizes, and in every color except blue.

Descriptions of flowering types range from pompom, peony-flowering, cactus, and more, but fall into two major categories: dwarf and tall. The dwarf forms range from 15 to 18 inches high and come in double and semi-double types. The tall varieties, wihch range from 2 to 6 feet high, are older and better for cutting. Unfortunately, they are also harder to find.

CULTIVATION

Dahlias are tender perennials, usually grown as annuals from seeds or tubers. Start seeds indoors 4 to 6 weeks before the last frost and move outdoors. Tubers should be planted directly in the garden. Dahlias can be planted in almost any type of soil, the ideal being neutral or slightly acidic. Plant in a sunny location under only one inch of soil with good drainage. Water and feed regularly, applying fertilizer monthly during the growing season. When the dahlia has three or four sets of leaves, pinch back once to grow a lower, bushier plant. Remove dead blooms for more flowering. In frost-free climates, tubers may be left in the ground. Otherwise, tubers must be lifted after frost and stored in a cool, dry place over the winter. Seeds are easier to handle, unless you don't mind digging up the tubers. But tubers offer the advantage of producing the same plant—seeds do not always come true in form and color to their parent plant. Dahlias make long-lasting cut flowers.

POSITION: Sun.

PROPAGATION: Seed, cuttings, or division.

Orange dahlia (left). White dahlia (right). Mixed dahlias (opposite).

Daylily

Common Daylily, *Hemerocallis fulva*
Lemon Lily, *H. lilio-asphodelus*

FOLKLORE

The daylily is native to Japan, China, and other parts of Asia. Cultivated as early as the twelfth century in China, they appear in paintings, on fabrics, and porcelain. The Chinese called the daylily the "plant of forgetfulness," because it was believed to cure sorrow by inducing memory loss. The plant was also used for relieving pain and cleansing the kidneys. The dried blossoms of the common daylily are often used in Chinese and Japanese cooking. Even today the Chinese eat unopened buds in salads.

Both common and lemon lilies were cultivated in England before 1597. One of the first flowers brought to America by the early colonists, daylilies were planted all over the east coast, including Williamsburg, where masses of them have continued to grow since colonial times. In 1890, new hybrids were introduced, and daylilies have enjoyed widespread popularity ever since.

The genus name *Hemerocallis* comes from two Greek words, *hemera* meaning "day" and *kallos*, "beautiful." The name aptly describes these lovely blooms that last for only a single day.

DESCRIPTION

The old-fashioned orange or tawny common daylily, *H. fulva,* grows 5 feet high, with trumpet-shaped flowers 3 to 4 inches long, rising above clumped foliage. The strap-like leaves grow 2 feet long and tend to arch. This daylily blooms in June and July and is a common sight along roadsides in midsummer.

Commonly called the lemon lily, *H. lilio-asphodelus* also blooms in June (sometimes late May) and July. Somewhat smaller than *H. fulva,* the plant grows only 2 to 3 feet high. The clumped foliage is similar to the common daylily, but the flowers are a beautiful pale yellow. Lemon lilies have a subtle fragrance and rarely grow outside the area where they were originally planted.

There are hundreds of daylily hybrids on the market, all descendants of the old-fashioned ones, and available in virtually every color but blue. Some are bi-colored. Clusters of up to 30 flower buds per stem open successively, each flower lasting only one day. It is possible, by careful selection, to have daylilies in bloom from May until September.

CULTIVATION

Daylilies are long-lasting perennials that grow in any ordinary, well-drained soil. They are easily established in locations that are dry and rocky, as well as in moist areas alongside streams or lakes.

Growing daylilies from seed is somewhat complicated. It is much easier to buy nursery plants in early spring or late summer. Plant in average soil, preferably with a lot of organic matter. Space dwarf varieties 18 inches apart and larger ones 24 to 36 inches apart.

Water in dry periods—the fleshy roots help daylilies withstand dry spells—and fertilize lightly. Too rich a soil encourages profuse foliage and few flowers. Divide every 5 or 6 years, in spring or late summer. Daylilies are long-lived and evergreen in mild climates.

POSITION: Sun or part shade.

PROPAGATION: Division or seed.

Naturalized daylilies (above). Lemon daylily (opposite).

Dianthus

Sweet William, *Dianthus barbatus*
Pinks, *D. deltoides*
Cottage Pinks, *D. plumarius*

FOLKLORE

The name *dianthus* means the "flower of Zeus," from the Greek *dios,* of Zeus, and *anthos,* flower. Sweet William was named after St. William of Aquitaine, and Pinks were named, aptly, for the pink and red shades of their blooms. A favorite for centuries, Sweet William was grown in the gardens of such notables as Henry VIII in the 1500s and Thomas Jefferson in 1767.

From early times, dianthus has been an important emblem. Soldiers of the Great Condé, the Prince de Héros (1621-1686) wore carnations to symbolize valour. French nobles wore them on their coats while attending executions. Napoleon chose the carnation-red color for the ribbon of the Legion of Honor. Since the Industrial Revolution, red carnations have symbolized socialism.

DESCRIPTION

These old-fashioned favorites are plants for everyone and every garden. All dianthus varieties make beautiful edgings plants for borders and look spectacular when planted in masses. Sweet Williams *(Dianthus barbatus)* are biennials that grow from 18 to 24 inches with blooms about the size of a nickel. They come in red, purple, white, and pink, as well as charming white-eyed types. Flowers are dense with a sweet fragrance. Sweet Williams bloom in late spring and early summer, and flower-last for five weeks or more. Pinks, also called Maiden pinks, *(D. deltoides)* are a low-growing, mat-forming species that grow 6 to 18 inches high. The flowers have a spicy fragrance. A perennial, they come in pink, white, red, and purple with slender blue-green leaves. Cottage Pinks *(D. plumarius),* a perennial with gray-green, grass-like leaves, grow 12 to 15 inches high. The flowers have fringed petals and bloom in abundance in May and June in red, rose, pink, or white.

CULTIVATION

Both annual and biennial dianthus grow well from seed, some flowering the first year. Perennial varieties are best started from nursery stock. Plant in neutral, well drained soil. Treat acidic soil with lime in early spring. Water moderately and fertilize in the spring and during flowering. Space plants 10 to 12 inches apart. Shear perennials back after flowering to encourage new growth. Mulch in the winter for protection against harsh weather. Dianthus self-sows readily if the soil around the plants is undisturbed. Dianthus is easy to grow from cuttings taken in the spring.

COMMENTS: Dianthus is considered annual, biennial, and perennial, depending on which book you consult and where you live. Most varieties are easily started from seed, but doubles should be started from cuttings. Pinks are the most fragrant and easiest to grow. Carnations *(D. caryophyllus)* are not as hardy as other varieties and are somewhat difficult to grow.

POSITION: Sun or light shade.

PROPAGATION: Seed, cuttings, division or layers.

Evening Primrose

Oenothera biennis

FOLKLORE

The evening primrose was sent from its native Virginia to Padua, Italy, in 1619. It was described by John Parkinson, King's Botanist to Charles I, as the "Prime-rose Tree" in his 1629 book on plants. Seventeenth-century gardeners called it the tree-primrose of Virginia, and other, more colorful names include donkey weed, gardener's bacon, and St. Anthony's ham.

Both the roots and leaves of the evening primrose are edible. Cultivated as a food in Germany and France for centuries, the roots and leaves are eaten either cooked or raw. In European folklore, the root of the evening primrose was thought to have the power to soothe vicious animals. Herbalists, too, favored the plant and used it as an antitoxin and as a curative for asthma and whooping cough.

Swedish botanist Carolus Linnaeus named the plant *Oenothera*, from the Greek *oinos*, "wine," and *thera*, "hunt" or "chase," because the root has a fragrance reminiscent of wine.

DESCRIPTION

Evening primrose is a dramatic plant in the garden, not only because of its beautiful, fragrant flowers, but also for its evening spectacle. Scores of night-flying moths and insects gather at dusk, just as the flowers unfold in the evening light, and a ballet of nature begins. The poet John Keats was "startled by the leap of buds into ripe flowers." The flowers are a clear, bright yellow, measure 3 inches across with a long flowering season, and bloom from early June to October. Flowers bloom for only one day, but new flowers take their place in succession. Plants eventually reach 3 to 4 feet.

CULTIVATION

Evening primrose is easy to raise from seed. Sow seeds in early spring directly in the garden or start indoors 6 to 8 weeks before setting out. Thin seedlings to 6 or 8 inches apart in any average, well-drained soil. Water only when soil is dry; fertilizer is rarely needed, if at all.

Evening primrose is a biennial plant that, once established, self-seeds with abandon. Plants look best when massed together in the front or middle of a border. Evening primrose is the perfect plant for the weekend gardener because it requires so little care and attention.

COMMENTS: The native Missouri primrose, *Oenothera missourensis*, is a perennial with 4-inch flowers that bloom on trailing stems during the day. The pink showy primrose, *O. speciosa*, is native to North American prairies. It grows wild along highways and in fields, and is often cultivated in Southwestern gardens.

POSITION: Sun or part shade.

PROPAGATION: Seed or cuttings.

Evening primrose (above). Missouri primrose (opposite).

Feverfew

Tanacetum parthenium

FOLKLORE

As its common name suggests, feverfew is a plant popular in American folk remedies. It was described in an old herbal book as an antidote for those "that have taken Opium too liberally," and was used as a poultice for wounds, or drunk with wine to counteract melancholy. It was also applied to ease toothaches and other minor pains. So versatile is feverfew in folk medicine, in fact, that it is often referred to as "housewife's aspirin."

In Europe, feverfew leaves are used in cooking, often tossed with other greens into salad, or wilted and chopped to season fried eggs. The scent is supposed to be particularly distasteful to bees and was said to keep away witches.

The species name *parthenium* was derived by the early botanists from a legend recounted by the Greek historian Plutarch (A.D. 46-120), wherein feverfew was used to save the life of a man who fell during the building of the Parthenon, and had gone "giddie in the head."

DESCRIPTION

An old-fashioned perennial with small, strongly-scented, daisy-like flowers, feverfew blooms profusely from early summer through fall over low, mounded forms. The flowers are 1 inch across and button-like, with short white petals emanating from yellow centers. The foliage is soft, green, hairy, and deeply cut, forming a low, spreading plant. Feverfew grows 12 to 15 inches high, but can reach 2 to 3 feet if it is not pinched back.

In warm climates, feverfew foliage remains evergreen. A lovely garden flower, feverfew is also beautiful in bouquets.

CULTIVATION

Feverfew tolerates most soils, but thrives in moist, well-drained soil enriched with organic matter. Plants bloom the first year from seed. Readily raised from seed, sow in the garden, but do not cover the seeds; light is essential for germination. Space plants 6 to 12 inches apart. There is no need to fertilize if organic matter has been added to the soil. Water during dry periods. Pinch back the plants when they grow 6 to 8 inches high to encourage bushier plants. Pinch back a second time before buds appear. Mulch for winter protection in cold climates. Single forms of feverfew self-sow prolifically, the double forms less so. Deadhead only to prevent the plant from self-sowing.

POSITION: Sun or part shade.

PROPAGATION: Seed.

Flax

Blue Flax
Linum perenne

FOLKLORE

Flax, a source of linen, has been cultivated for millenia. Pharaohs found in tombs some 4,000 years old are mummified in unguents applied to wraps of linen made from flax. Later cultures of the Egyptian, Chinese, Greek, Peruvian, Spanish, Welsh, German, and Roman peoples used flax for its fiber as well as for the oil that is extracted from flax seed. Today, the oil is used in paints, inks, soaps, and linoleum.

Native Americans made use of every part of the blue flax. Seeds were roasted and eaten alone or as a condiment in soups and stews. Seeds were also crushed to make meal, or processed into oil. Flax fibers were made into fishing lines and ropes. Blue flax was also highly regarded for its medicinal properties, and was used to relieve rheumatism, coughs, colds, and lung congestions. A tea of steeped stems was drunk to cure stomach problems. Poultices of flax fibers were used to reduce swelling from burns. American pioneers, who often learned practices from the Native Americans, used a similar poultice mixed with corn meal for wounds or to reduce the swelling caused by mumps.

Prized for its ornamental value, blue flax is still grown in colonial Williamsburg.

DESCRIPTION

This splendid plant is unrivalled in its ability to brighten up borders, with its brilliant, sky-blue hues. Flowers, 1-inch wide, bloom in great profusion on delicate, airy stems that reach 12 to 18 inches high. Although most varieties are blue, some have white flowers. The leaves are blue-green, narrow, and pointed. The blooms open only in early sunshine and close by early afternoon. Flowers will not open in the shade. This old-fashioned perennial blooms from mid-spring to mid-summer and is most often seen in meadow gardens, where it naturalizes well.

CULTIVATION

Blue flax is easy to grow from seed and will bloom the first year if sown in early spring. Seeds are readily available, but young plants at nurseries are rarely seen. Sow seeds outdoors after frost or start indoors 4 weeks before putting out. Any average, well-drained soil is adequate, but plants will thrive in light, moderately fertile, sandy soil. Space 12 to 18 inches apart and water regularly. When flowering is over, cut plants back to 6 inches; the plant may bloom again. Although they are not long-lived, usually only 3 to 4 years, blue flax plants are easily resown and often self-sow.

COMMENTS: *L. p. lewisii*, native to the west coast, is better suited to that area than *L. perenne*. The annual *L. grandiflorum*, scarlet flax, has red flowers and is particularly tolerant of hot and dry conditions, making it an excellent choice for warmer climates.

POSITION: Sun.

PROPAGATION: Seed or division.

Forget-Me-Not

Myosotis sylvatica

FOLKLORE

Tradition tells us that when God was naming the plants and animals of the earth, a little flower raised its sweet head to heaven and prayed to the Lord to be remembered. The prayer was heard and the little flower henceforth was called forget-me-not.

A French knight, walking with his lady love beside a river, knelt to gather the flowers that grew along the bank. But the ground was slippery and his footing unsure. The knight fell and, from the weight of his armor, he sank deep into the rushing current—but not before he threw the flowers to his maiden, urging her to "forget-me-not." Yet another legend tells of an angel who fell in love with a mortal and was not let back into heaven until forget-me-nots were planted all over the earth.

Henry of Lancaster, later Henry IV, took the forget-me-not as his personal emblem, never wanting to be forgotten wherever he went. The poet Samuel Taylor Coleridge immortalized the flower in his poem "The Keepsake," written in 1817.

The genus name *Myosotis* is from the Greek *mys*, "mouse," and *ous*, "ear," probably because the leaves resemble mouse ears.

DESCRIPTION

These lovely azure flowers are a delight in the garden, blooming generously in early spring when the first tree leaves come out. The delicate, tiny flowers are usually blue with a yellow eye, but also come in pink or white, and form clusters of ¼-inch flowers. The low-growing, mound-shaped plants reach 8 to 12 inches high and 10 inches wide. Multibranched stems produce an abundance of flowers.

Forget-me-nots will naturalize in cool, moist conditions along streams and riverbanks. A biennial often treated as an annual, it makes an excellent ground cover for spring-blooming bulbs and is exquisite in bouquets.

CULTIVATION

Ordinary soil will do, but forget-me-nots thrive in fertile, moist, rich soil. Partial shade is best, but plants tolerate full sun.

Sow seeds in late summer or early fall for a bountiful array of flowers the next spring, blooming the same time as daffodils and tulips. Forget-me-nots can also be sown in early spring for late summer bloom, or they can be started indoors 4 to 6 weeks before setting out in early spring.

Keep well watered—plants will perform even in wet soil—and fertilize every 4 to 6 weeks. Forget-me-nots reseed abundantly, and perform vigorously year after year, particularly in regions where the springtime is cool.

POSITION: Part shade or sun.

PROPAGATION: Seed or divison.

Four O'Clock

Marvel of Peru

Mirabilis jalapa

FOLKLORE

Four o'clock seeds were brought from the Peruvian Andes to Spain in the sixteenth century and have been grown in European gardens since 1540. The flower takes its common name from its afternoon behavior. When in bloom, flowers open at approximately four o'clock each day and remain open all night.

Beautiful as well as reliable, four o'clocks are also revered for their elegance and fragrance. These qualities are celebrated in the French name for the flower, *belle de nuit*, or "beauty of the night."

Like so many old-fashioned flowers, four o'-clocks have been put to practical use. In the Malay Archipelago, four o'clocks are said to be so habitual in their opening time that they are planted to serve as house clocks. The Japanese grind the seeds into a cosmetic powder and the Chinese use the flower pigment to dye seaweed gelatins. Roots from the native Arizona four o'clocks were chewed by the Hopi Indians to alter moods. Zuni women made a powder from the roots to relieve indigestion and other pains caused by overeating.

Thomas Jefferson was charmed by their strong fragrance and planted four o'clocks in the front gardens near the windows at Monticello.

DESCRIPTION

Four o'clocks are one of those old-fashioned plants rarely seen in gardens today. With their incredible fragrance, they are enchanting when planted near a terrace, under windows, or in containers set near patio furniture. Although the flowers fold up during the bright sunlight hours, they will open like clockwork in the late afternoon and remain open all night. They are irresistible to many kinds of night-flying moths.

On cloudy days, four o'clocks stay open most of the day. The trumpet-shaped flowers grow 1 to 2 inches long in red, yellow, violet, and white. Some varieties have spotted or striped flowers. The rounded, shrub-like plants grow 2 to 3½ feet.

CULTIVATION

Sow seeds indoors 6 weeks before the last frost or plant directly in the garden. Sow plants in peat pots to minimize transplanting shock. Space 12 inches apart in light, well-drained soil, although four o'clocks will tolerate poor soil. Keep well watered and fertilize regularly. Four o'clocks self-sow readily. Their tuberous roots can be dug up in the fall, stored over the winter, and replanted to produce even larger flowers the next season. Four o'clocks are resistant to heat and air pollution.

COMMENTS: Four o'clocks make a good temporary hedge.

POSITION: Sun or light shade.

PROPAGATION: Seed.

Foxglove

Digitalis purpurea

FOLKLORE

The lore surrounding foxglove is copious. It ranges from classical mythology to fairy tales, and embraces themes from fertility to fairies' pranks. For example:

The Roman goddess Juno, upset that Jupiter created Minerva without a mother, determined she would create a fatherless offspring. Juno sought the advice of the goddess Flora, who told her of the magical powers of a meadow flower certain to aid Juno's plan. Upon touching the foxglove, Juno immediately conceived the baby Mars.

Wicked fairies were always playing pranks on mortals. Once they decided to help the wily foxes invade the chicken houses. The fairies slipped foxgloves over the ravenous mammals' paws. Now, ever so quietly, the begloved foxes slipped into the coops and gobbled the contents. As evidence of their collusion, the mischievous fairies left their fingerprints in the form of tiny spots on the foxglove blossoms.

The genus name *Digitalis* was first given to the plant in the sixteenth century because the shape of the flowers resemble the fingers of gloves. Foxglove is a source of digitalin, a drug still used today to treat heart disease.

DESCRIPTION

One of the finest of old-fashioned garden flowers, foxglove's stately spires of bloom tower 3 to 4 feet above basal clumps of dark green leaves. The long spikes are densely covered with flowers of pink, white, cream, rose, crimson, or yellow, all with spotted throats. The flowers, which resemble small thimbles or bells, are about 2 inches long and bloom in late spring and early summer. The lower blooms may continue to bloom sporadically all summer.

Plant foxgloves in small groups or drifts in a border, or blend them with columbine, bleeding heart, and ferns.

CULTIVATION

Foxglove, a biennial, is readily raised from seed sown in early summer for blooms the next year. Once established, foxglove often reseeds itself every year. For blooms in the planting year, purchase second year plants, which are available at most nurseries.

Flowers last for at least six weeks. Set plants 1 to 1½ feet apart in an acidic, rich, well-drained soil. Keep seedlings moist and fertilize regularly. Cut off the flower stems immediately after blooming; the plant will strengthen, produce more rosettes, and bloom with even more flowers the next year.

Use a loose, airy mulch; plants tend to rot if a heavy mulch is used around the base.

COMMENTS: *D. lutea*, a somewhat smaller plant, has creamy yellow flowers. *D.* x *mertonensis* are perennial varieties, with rose or red flowers.

POSITION: Part shade.

PROPAGATION: Seed.

Gaillardia

Blanket Flower, *Gaillardia pulchella*

FOLKLORE

The novelist Willa Cather described the Nebraskan prairies as fields where gaillardias "matted over the ground with the deep velvety red that is in Bokhara carpets." A native flower of North America, its range encompasses much of the central United States, including the plains of Oklahoma, Texas, Nebraska, Missouri, Kansas, and Colorado.

Gaillardia is commonly called blanket flower because some say its grey, woolly leaves resemble soft blankets.

Native American artisans may also have inspired the common name; the flowers are depicted in many of the brightly-colored blanket designs woven by the Plains Indians. But the Indian blankets surely inspired the name of a recently introduced variety—Indian Chief.

Despite its French name—after Gaillard de Marentonneau, an eighteenth-century botanist—gaillardia is native to North America.

DESCRIPTION

Gaillardias are tender perrenials usually treated as annuals. They grow in mounds 15 to 24 inches high. Strong stems support dark green, hairy foliage with either single or double blooms in red, bronze, yellow, burgundy, or combinations of these colors. The daisy-like flowers are 2½ to 4 inches in diameter, with centers of dark reddish-brown. They have an exceptionally long flowering period, from June through late autumn, and provide welcome color in the fall garden. Gaillardias prefer heat and tolerate winds, and are especially easy to grow in areas with little rainfall or in seaside gardens.

CULTIVATION

Gaillardias provide long-lasting color for little maintenance. Simply plant where sun is abundant and in an open position.

Gaillardias perform best in light, sandy, well-drained soil, but will tolerate most any soils, except clay. For early blooms, sow seed indoors 4 to 6 weeks before the last frost or start directly in the garden in warm soil. Light is essential for germination, so barely cover the seed. Space at least 12 to 18 inches apart to allow plants to spread. Fertilize little, if at all. Water occasionally, except during periods of drought.

Remove flowers as they fade to prolong bloom. Plants occasionally self-seed.

COMMENTS: Not reliable in wet and cold climates.

POSITION: Sun.

PROPAGATION: Seed, division, or cuttings.

Common gaillardia (above). *Gaillardia pulchella* 'Red Plume' (opposite).

Geranium

Pelargonium species

FOLKLORE

The people of the Mediterranean claim the origin of the geranium. According to legend, once, when the prophet Mohammed washed his shirt, he laid it to dry on a mallow plant. When he took his shirt to dress again, the mallow had been transformed into a brilliant geranium.

The first geraniums sent to Holland came from South Africa in 1609. By 1650, the plants were common in Europe, where they were grown for their beauty as well as for their fragrance. By the mid-1700s, perfumeries were cultivating geraniums for commercial use. In the United States, Thomas Jefferson grew the geranium as a houseplant both at the President's house (later the White House) and at Monticello. Upon leaving the Presidency, Jefferson gave geranium plants as a parting gifts to friends. But, during the Victorian era, geraniums enjoyed their greatest popularity as a bedding and indoor plant.

The geranium was so named because it was similar to the wild geranium growing in many areas of Europe, and was erroneously classified as a geranium. The genus Geranium has entirely different characteristics.

DESCRIPTION

The common geranium, *P. x horturum* or zonal geranium, is a bedding plant that comes in single- or double-flower varieties. The flowers form 5- to 7-inch round clusters atop leafless stems. The heartshaped leaves have scalloped edges, some with dark marking called "zoning," some solid green, and others variegated. Flowers bloom in red, pink, rose, salmon, lavender, and white on plants reaching 18 to 24 inches high. Trailing geraniums can reach up to 3 feet in length and are excellent in containers and hanging baskets. The scented geraniums are especially nice, but not as well known; grow them for the lemon, rose, apple, and mint scents of their leaves. Geraniums are grown as annuals.

CULTIVATION

It's far simpler to purchase geranium plants than to start them from seed. Starting seed is not difficult, it just takes a long time—10 to 15 weeks before they're ready to plant in the garden. If you do sow seeds, barely cover them with soil and keep them in a warm spot (70° to 80°F). Set seedlings outdoors after the last frost, 8 to 12 inches apart, in rich, well-drained, and slightly acid soil. Fertilize monthly (containers bi-weekly) and keep well watered. Cut off faded blooms to encourage more flowering. Geraniums are perennial in frost-free areas. They are extremely easy to propagate from cuttings taken in August or September. Overwinter them indoors, and put them out in spring after frost.

COMMENTS: *P. x horturum*, are common geraniums, and *P. peltatum*, are ivy or trailing geraniums. *P. x domesticum*, called regal geraniums, bear large flowers and can only be grown in cool areas.

POSITION: Sun or part shade.

PROPAGATION: Seed or cuttings.

Geranium x *hortorum* 'Freckles' (above). Common geranium (opposite).

Gladiola

Sword Lily

Gladiolus

FOLKLORE

In classical mythology, when Apollo accidentally slew his friend Hyancinthus, gladiolas sprang from the spilt blood. Consequently, gladiolas are often associated with grief.

In folk tradition, young men wore gladiolas to the marriages of their friends to represent the parting of their youth and boyhood affection. Gladiolas are also thought to be the "lilies of the field" that Jesus referred to in the Sermon on the Mount, for these flowers grew wild in the Holy Land.

First introduced to England from Turkey in 1620 by John Tradescant, Sr., the gardener to King Charles I, gladiolas were immediately popular in formal and cottage gardens. Many new species were developed in the eighteenth century, and in 1807, when the first known hybrid was produced, gladiolas were in particular demand. It was a favorite in Victorian and Edwardian gardens and in the Victorian *Language of Flowers*, the gladiola represents strength of character .

The name *Gladiolus* is from the Latin *gladius*, meaning "small sword," which describes the shape of the foliage.

DESCRIPTION

Gladiolas were at one time the most popular of all garden flowers. Their decline was most likely due to overuse, but they remain a magnificent, long-lasting cut flower. Gladiolas can be grown easily in all parts of the United States and can be grown year round in southern climates. Select early, midseason, and late varieties, to extend the growing season. There is a tremendous number of gladiolas from which to choose, in every color except blue, some with bi-colors. Flowers are elegant spikes that grow in a narrow, upright habit. Individual flowers range in size from 2½ to 5½ inches wide. Blooms last only a week but a single stalk can last several weeks. Plants bloom midsummer to frost. Gladiolas make a long-lasting cut flower.

CULTIVATION

Gladiolas grow from a corm, often erroneously called a bulb. Plant corms in early spring as soon as the soil can be worked. Gladiolas thrive in almost any soil of medium fertility, and do best in well-drained, sandy loam. Plant corms 2 to 6 inches deep, depending on the type, and space 3 to 6 inches apart. If planting in rows, space rows 18 to 24 inches apart. When planting, fertilize beneath the corm, making sure that fertilizer does not touch the corm. Water plentifully and mulch to conserve moisture. For cut flowers, cut the spikes when the first flowers start to open, leaving four or five leaves on the plant to produce next year's growth. Snip off faded blooms. For successive bloom, plant every two weeks until midsummer. To eliminate staking, plant an inch or two deeper. Corms will need to be lifted as soon as the foliage has turned yellow, and stored for the winter in a frostproof cellar. Gladiolas can remain in the ground in Zones 8 to 10. Since gladiolas do not come true from seed, they are usually not propagated this way.

COMMENTS: *G. byzantinus*, a very old species introduced from Turkey in 1629, is a spring-flowering gladiola that is less well known but very old-fashioned. It is hardier than most, and ideal for naturalizing.

POSITION: Sun or light shade.

PROPAGATION: Division.

Gladiolus byzantinus (above). Garden gladiolas (opposite).

Heliotrope

Cherry Pie Plant
Heliotropium arborescens

FOLKLORE

In Greek mythology, the nymph Clytie, who had died for love of the sun-god Apollo, was transformed into a heliotrope and her flower head forever thereafter followed the sun. The name *Heliotropium* is Greek for a flower that constantly turns its face toward the sun.

Heliotropes were introduced to Europe from Peru in 1757 by Joseph de Jussieu, who sent it to France and was said to have been "intoxicated with delight" by its perfume. Heliotrope immediately became popular on the continent and was called *Herbe d'amour*, or "Flower of Love." *The Language of Flowers* describes it as "eternal love." A favorite of the Victorians, heliotropes were used extensively as bedding plants.

In 1786, Thomas Jefferson sent heliotrope seeds to North America from France. He grew the flowers at his home in Virginia. George Washington and Andrew Jackson also grew heliotropes in their gardens. One of the oldest common names given to heliotrope, cherry pie plant, is of British origin. Evidently, they found the smell to be like cherry pie fresh out of the oven.

Throughout history, heliotropes have been widely used for perfume. In lore, they are supposed to cure warts and have been used as a cure for sore throats. Heliotropes have also been made into an astringent, and are valued for their tannic properties.

DESCRIPTION

The powerful, sweet scent of heliotropes demands that these wonderful plants be placed near a frequently used window or on a porch. The scent is often likened to vanilla, sliced apples, or warm cherry pie. Depending on the variety, plants grow 18 to 30 inches high and produce large clusters of tiny flowers in deep purple, lilac, or white. Flower bunches can be as wide as 15 inches across. The textured, dark green foliage can be made bushier by topping, or pinching back, the plants. Heliotropes bloom profusely from June through first frost.

CULTIVATION

Heliotropes are tender perennials, usually grown as annuals. Start seed indoors 10 to 12 weeks before the last frost. Heliotropes are very sensitive to frost, so be sure to set plants out after all danger has passed. Barely push the seed into the soil to allow light to aid germination. Be patient; germination can take up to three or four weeks. Space plants approximately 10 to 12 inches apart in rich, well-drained soil high in organic matter. Water moderately and fertilize monthly. If growing in pots or containers, place plants in part shade and fertilize more frequently.

COMMENTS: Heliotropes do very well as container plants. Bring pots in before the first frost. Place them in an area with cool (60°F) nights and they will bloom all winter. Be careful not to overwater this plant—the perfume tends to increase in slightly dry soil.

POSITION: Sun or part shade.

PROPAGATION: Seed.

Hibiscus

Rose Mallow
Hibiscus moscheutos

FOLKLORE

In Polynesian tradition, a woman who wears one red hibiscus flower behind her left ear is saying "I desire a lover"; if the flower is worn behind her right ear, she is saying "I have a lover"; and behind both ears, "I have one lover, but desire another."

Hibiscus is an ingredient in cooking and medicine. The seed capsules are served as a vegetable or used as a seasoning in soups and stews, the leaves in casseroles and omelets. Hibiscus was also used in cough remedies and to ease internal pains.

Hibiscus, often called rose mallow, is native to the eastern United States, and has naturalized from Massachusetts to Florida and inland to the Great Lakes. Other common names include swamp mallow or sea hollyhock.

Hibiscus is the ancient Greek name given to the flower, and is the name at, since ancient Virgil called the mallow. The name hibiscus may have been derived from the ibis, a bird that since ancient times has shared the marshy habitats where hibiscus flourishes.

DESCRIPTION

With its large showy blooms, attractive foliage, and unusually vigorous growth, hibiscus is spectacular in the garden from mid-July to September. The saucer-shaped flowers are very large, up to 8 to 10 inches across, and come in rose, pink, crimson, or white. The foliage is bold and dense, with 8-inch leaves. The plants grow as tall as 5 feet. Although hibiscus flowers last for only one day, an abundance of new blooms appear regularly. When in bloom, they are always covered with flowers. Hibiscus are most effective when planted in large groups or alone in a mass planting.

CULTIVATION

This tender perennial is very easy to grow from seed, and flowers the first year if started indoors early in the season, about 8 weeks before the last frost. Soak the seeds overnight or notch the seeds for faster germination. Seeds may be sown directly in the garden in spring, and will bloom the next year. Space seedlings 24 to 36 inches apart, ideally in moist, rich soil; hibiscus will perform in ordinary garden soil, even soggy soil. Water abundantly in dry soils and fertilize regularly for larger, lusher plants. Despite their height, hibiscus's thick, sturdy stems rarely need staking. Once established, they are long-lived. Hibiscus can be divided in spring or fall and are marginally hardy in northern gardens beyond Zone 6.

COMMENTS: *H. coccineus*, the scarlet mallow, is a perennial also native to North America. It has beautiful crimson flowers and deeply divided leaves. The plant typically called the Rose of Sharon (*H. syriacus*) is a shrub hibiscus.

POSITION: Sun or part shade.

PROPAGATION: Seed, division, or cuttings.

Hibiscus 'Disco Bell' and begonias (above). *Hibiscus* 'Disco Bell' (opposite).

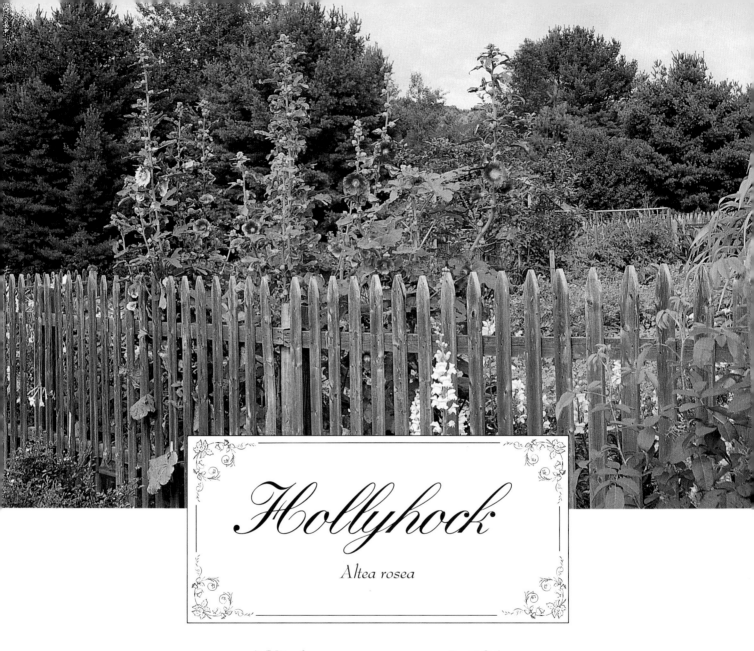

Hollyhock

Altea rosea

FOLKLORE

Hollyhocks have been popular for centuries. Originally cultivated in China during the fifth or sixth century, they are a recurring motif in delicate Chinese paintings. They have been grown extensively in England since the fifteenth century, and by 1850, no English garden was without a collection. Popular throughout Europe, they were particular favorites of Goethe, and were painted by Renoir and other Impressionists. Brought to the Americas by European settlers, hollyhocks quickly became a regular sight in colonial gardens.

The hollyhock is native to the Near East and is thought to have been brought to Europe with the returning Crusaders. The name was originally holy-hock, which may have been given it by the Crusaders. It took its name probably because the plant was thought to cure illnesses, among them lung diseases and tuberculosis. Hollyhock was also believed to relieve bladder diseases.

DESCRIPTION

No old-fashioned garden is complete without the imperial hollyhock. Tall, stately plants vary in height from 5 to 8 feet and support flowers up to 4 inches across in pink, crimson, yellow, cream, or white, in double and single varieties. A biennial often grown as an annual, hollyhocks bloom from July through September. Once planted, hollyhocks usually reseed themselves. The large, maple-like leaves look especially nice planted against a wall or a fence, or used as a foundation plant.

CULTIVATION

Readily raised from seed, hollyhocks are best treated as biennials. Start seeds early in February or March indoors to produce flowers the first year. Soak seeds overnight to hasten germination, and barely cover the seeds. After final frost, place the crowns of the plants a little below the soil surface and space 12 to 15 inches apart. Seeds may be sown outside in early summer for blooms the following year. Average soil is adequate, but hollyhocks thrive in deeply dug, fertile soil. Water and fertilize regularly. After flowering, cut stems down to the base to prolong the life of the plant. Hollyhocks need staking to prevent damage in windy weather.

COMMENTS: Hollyhocks self-sow but seed does not often come true to variety.
It's best to purchase new plants or start new seeds.

POSITION: Sun or light shade.

PROPAGATION: Seed, division, or cuttings.

Honesty

Money plant
Lunaria annua

FOLKLORE

Honesty may have more common names than any other plant, among them white satin, satin-flower, pennyflower, silverplate, prick-song-woort, judas pence, shillings, two-pennies-in-a-purse, and money-in-both-pockets. All of these names refer to the form and color of the seed pods, which are flat, moon-like disks.

Because of the curious seed pods, honesty became a favorite in medieval gardens. Enjoyed through the centuries, honesty reached the pinnacle of its popularity among the Victorians, who grew the plants in their drawing rooms. On dull winter days, Victorian women spent their leisure time painstakingly hand painting the translucent seed pods. These silvery disks have been used for winter decorations from the mid-eighteenth century to this day.

Originally cultivated in Sweden in 1570, honesty was used by doctors to dress wounds and to treat epilepsy. The roots have been eaten in salads since the 1500s. Honesty was very popular in colonial America; its seeds were widely offered for sale, and were found growing in the gardens at Mount Vernon and Monticello.

The seed pods, which resemble little moons, inspired the genus name *Lunaria*.

DESCRIPTION

Grown primarily for its curious-looking seed pods, honesty grows 2½ to 3 feet high and bears single, rosy-violet or white, four-petaled flowers. The spring-blooming flowers—often overlooked because of the interest in the decorative pods—should not be discounted. Flowers bloom from May until July. The dark green leaves are toothed and slightly sweet-scented. The moon-shaped seed pods appear green at first, then turn a translucent silvery color. Grow honesty in large groups or informal masses for best effect.

CULTIVATION

Honesty is hardy and undemanding. It grows in average garden soil or even in rather poor, dry soil. Once planted, try not to disturb the plants, as they are not easily transplanted. Simple to grow from seed sown indoors in March, honesty seedlings should be set out in the spring, approximately 10 to 12 inches apart. If grown as a biennial, plant directly in the garden in early summer for flowers the following spring. Water only moderately and fertilize once a year, if at all. A prolific self-seeder, honesty will sprout and bloom abundantly each year.

COMMENTS: For dried flowers, cut the seed pods as soon as the green fades. Hang upside down until thoroughly dry. If handled with care, the pods will last several years.

POSITION: Part shade.

PROPAGATION: Seed.

Iris

Purple Iris, Flag Iris, *Iris germanica*
Siberian iris, *I. sibirica*

🌿 FOLKLORE 🌿

One of the oldest cultivated plants, the iris was among the flowers brought back to Egypt by Thutmosis III (1501-1447 B.C.) after he conquered Syria. It was also one of the flowers he had painted on his elaborate temple at Karnak. To the ancient Egyptians, the iris symbolized eloquence. The Egyptians, as well as the Romans and Moors, prized the iris for its medicinal qualities. It was also used in cosmetics and, at one time, was widely used in the manufacture of perfume (the rhizomes, when dried, contain a violet-like scent).

The iris called yellow water-flag (*I. pseudacorus*) is regarded as the origin of the French *fleur-de-lis*. In A.D. 496, when the army of the French king Clovis I was trapped by the Goths, Clovis saw the yellow iris growing far out in a river and realized it was shallow enough for his army to cross to safety. In appreciation, he adopted the flower as his emblem. After the Crusades, it was called the *fleur de Louis*, after Louis VII.

The iris is named for the goddess Iris, the messenger of Juno. The rainbow was her bridge between heaven and earth. The Greek word *iris* means "eye of heaven," and refers to the rainbow.

DESCRIPTION

The tall bearded iris (*I. germanica*), also known as the German iris, most commonly seen on roadsides and in old gardens, is purple, although its hybrids come in every color. The principal characteristic is a "beard" at the base of the outer petals, often appearing in a color different from the standard petals. Old-fashioned favorites are known for their fragrance; bearded iris have a sweet subtle scent. They grow 1 to 3 feet high with sword-like foliage and bloom in May and June.

Another easy, popular iris is the Siberian iris (*I. sibirica*). It is one of the hardiest of flowers, and was grown before 1597. The plants have slender grass-like foliage with rigid upright stems, and produce smaller flowers than the bearded iris. Blooms come mostly in shades of dark purple. Thriving in almost any moderately moist soil, they are ideal for naturalizing or for growing on the edges of ponds and streams.

CULTIVATION

One of the oldest of garden plants, iris is extremely easy and requires minimum attention. Plant rhizomes just below the soil surface in any well-drained, light soil amended with a reasonable amount of well-rotted manure. Fertilize annually with bone meal or superphosphate. Do not overwater. This type of iris likes it dry; water only during drought. Iris grows fast and should be divided every 3 to 5 years. Division should be done just after flowering. If disturbed in the fall or spring, plants may not bloom the next season. Iris can be raised by seed, but germination is poor. Propagation is easier by division. Provide a winter mulch in cold climates. The Siberian iris requires a rich, moist soil and, if watered regularly, will produce larger and more plentiful flowers.

COMMENTS: *I. pseudacorus*, *I. daempferi*, *I. laevigata*, *I. fulva*, and *I. menniesii* require boggy conditions or shallow water, making them suitable for ponds. *I. orentialis* performs best in hot summers and exists on little moisture, making it perfect for warmer climates.

POSITION: Sun or part shade.

PROPAGATION: Division or seed.

Tall bearded iris (above). Siberian iris (opposite).

Lily

Lilium species

❧ FOLKLORE ❧

For thousands of years, the lily has symbolized purity and beauty in literature and art. The Madonna lily, *L. candidum*, is considered the oldest domesticated flower, and is associated with the Blessed Virgin because of its pure white color and rich perfume. This is the lily most often depicted in the paintings of the masters, and is the only flower that Jesus mentioned by name. The Madonna lily is named and described by Virgil, Chaucer, Shakespeare, and others.

Another renowned old-fashioned lily is the tiger lily, *L. tigrinum*. Its bright orange color inspired its common name. Grown as a field crop in China, Korea, and Japan, it is edible. In Lewis Carroll's *Alice's Adventures in Wonderland*, the tiger lily lures Alice into the looking-glass garden.

Around 1900, there was a mad craze for growing lilies in Europe, but the mosaic virus destroyed plants as well as the passion. Tiger lilies remained popular, however, because they survived the disease.

DESCRIPTION

Lilies are among the most beautiful and ornamental garden flowers. The Madonna lily has long been cherished for its pure white and very fragrant blooms. The trumpet-shaped flowers are large, up to 3 inches long, with many blooms on each stem. The tiger lily blooms deep orange with 4-inch flowers on stems growing to 5 feet. The old-fashioned varieties bloom in June and early July, on stems reaching 3 to 5 feet. Continuous bloom is possible by planting a variety of the multitudes of new lilies now available. Lilies come in a variety of shades of white, yellow, orange, red, and lavender.

CULTIVATION

Most lilies are hardy and require little care, provided bulbs are purchased from virus-free stock from a reliable source. Lilies prefer slightly acid or neutral soil. Heavy clay and sandy soils will need a generous amount of humus . Good drainage is essential—bulbs will rot if left in damp areas. Bulbs should be planted in the fall at least one full month before the ground freezes. Depth of planting the bulbs varies with different types of lilies. *L. candidum* and *l. giganteum* need only an inch or two of soil cover; others need 6 to 8 inches of soil cover. Lilies should remain in place; avoid tranplanting until they get crowded. Water regularly if drought occurs and mulch to conserve moisture. Fertilize once a year in early fall or early spring. Let the leaves turn yellow and die away gradually. Stems can be cut down to 2 feet above ground in the fall and totally removed in early spring.

POSITION: Sun or part shade.
PROPAGATION: Seeds or bulbs.

Turkcap lily (above). Lily hybrid (opposite).

Lily of the Valley

Convallaria majalis

FOLKLORE

In ancient times, the lily of the valley was considered the special flower of Ostara, the Norse Goddess of the Dawn. Through the ages, the flower came to be called Our Lady's tears because it was said to grow where Mary shed tears at the foot of the cross. In Irish lore, the flowers are called fairy ladders because it was thought that "little people" climbed them. The poet John Keats called it the queen of flowers, and its beauty and sweet fragrance has been celebrated by many other poets, including Percy Shelley and Sir Walter Scott.

Lily of the valley has strong associations with medicine. The British horticulturist Henry Lyte stated in his *New Herbal* (1578) that the water of the flowers strengthen the memory and restore it to its natural vigor. Lily of the valley was once believed to cure gout, and was used as a heart tonic. It was even used as an ingredient of love potions. The leaves and flowers produce a drug used medicinally today.

The name lily of the valley comes from *convallis*, "valley," a typical habitat for the flower. Convallis inspired alternate names including conval lily or wood lily.

DESCRIPTION

Among the loveliest scented flowers, the lily of the valley has graceful spikes of little bell-shaped flowers that dangle among bright green, lance-shaped leaves. Blooms are usually white, but newer forms also come in pink and double. Flowers last from late April to late May, according to climate, and grow to about 10 inches high. The foliage thrives all summer, making a nice groundcover. In late summer, attractive bright red berries appear. Lily of the valley has one of the most intoxicating of fragrances; pick a flower and sniff it all day long.

CULTIVATION

Although easy to grow, lily of the valley does not easily transplant. Purchase rhizomes (often called pips) and plant them where they will stay in the garden. Once established, they are long-lasting and require little care. Planting is best done in late September or October in a cool, shaded position in moderately rich soil. Enrich with rotted manure annually in the spring. Try to keep the plants relatively moist by mulching. The plants will increase rapidly by creeping rootstock. Lily of the valley is a perfect plant for a shady north exposure or under trees.

COMMENTS: An excellent cut flower, Lily of the valley is especially lovely in a small bouquet, or when used to scent a room delicately, or as a boutonniere or corsage. M. rosea is the pink form and M. flore plena is a double form. The white underground stems are poisonous.

POSITION: Part shade or full shade.

PROPAGATION: Division of clumps or rhizomes.

Love-in-a-Mist

Nigella damascena

FOLKLORE

Love-in-a-mist takes its name from the misty-looking collar of thin, lacey bracts that surround the flower. This unusual collar has inspired numerous other common names, including devil-in-a-bush, jack-in-the-green, lady-in-the-bower, and fennel flower.

Nigellas were mentioned by the Greek philosopher and botanist Theophrastus as early as 300 B.C. and by the plant historian Dioscorides about 500 A.D. First grown for medicinal uses, love-in-a-mist was particularly sought for stomach disorders and fevers. The seeds were also valued in cooking and used for their nutmeg-like flavoring. In Egypt, the seeds have been sprinkled on breads and cakes since the time of the Pharoahs. From early Tudor times, English bakers imported love-in-a-mist seeds from Egypt to garnish their own breads and cakes.

Thomas Jefferson grew nigella as early as 1810, and Celia Thaxter, gardener and author of *The Island Garden*, delighted in this "old-fashioned flower" in her island garden off New Hampshire in 1893.

The genus name comes from *niger*, "black," for the color of its seeds.

DESCRIPTION

Love-in-a-mist is a suitably alluring name for this lovely flower. Blooms grow 1 1/2 inches across, usually in sky blue, but also in white or pink. Stems are erect and branching. The delicate foliage is divided into fine, lace-like segments, which create an illusion of flowers floating against a mist of bright green leaves. The plant grows 12 to 30 inches high and blooms in early summer, longer if planted successively. The seed pods form a pale green capsule just beneath the flat flower, and make an interesting addition to cut flower arrangements or to dried everlastings.

CULTIVATION

Love-in-a-mist is easy to cultivate and it naturalizes freely from self-sown seed. It thrives in any soil, even the poorest, but does best in sandy, moderately dry soil with good drainage. Sow directly in position as soon as the ground can be worked. The long tap roots make transplanting difficult, although seeds can be sown indoors 4 to 6 weeks ahead in peat pots to minimize transplanting shock. Seeds can be sown in autumn in mild climates for earlier flowering the next spring. Thin to 6 to 8 inches, fertilize monthly, and water only when the soil is dry. The flowering season is short, but successive plantings made every two weeks from early spring until June will provide continuous summer bloom. Once grown, love-in-a-mist will usually re-seed successively for years.

POSITION: Sun.

PROPAGATION: Seed.

Love-Lies-Bleeding

Amaranthus caudatus

FOLKLORE

Love-lies-bleeding takes its common name from its long, crimson flowers. Other delightful common names are tassel flower, and kiss-me-over-the-garden-gate. In France, the blood-red blooms are known by the gruesome name nun's scourge.

Native to India and South America, love-lies-bleeding has been a popular garden plant since the sixteenth century. It has been referred to by a number of poets, including John Milton, who called it the "immortal amaranth," and by Edmund Spencer, who dubbed it the "sad amaranthus." In *The*

Language of Flowers, the flower symbolizes the hopeless and heartless, but many regard it as the flower of love because of its deep red color.

Love-lies-bleeding has had a long history in the Americas as well. The Aztecs considered it of great importance. Flowers were used for ceremonial purposes. The seeds, known as Inca wheat, filled granaries throughout the Aztec empire. Early settlers brought the seed to North America, and grew them as medicinal herbs in the mistaken belief that the leaves would stop bleeding.

DESCRIPTION

Brilliant plants with bright green foliage, love-lies-bleeding have some of the most unusual flowers ever seen. Blooms in spiked clusters hang in drooping crimson plumes up to 2 feet long. These showy tassels adorn upright plants that grow 3 to 5 feet, and spread about 2 feet. The bright, bold color of love-lies-bleeding demands space, so give it plenty of room for best effect. A tender annual, it blooms in summer and lasts until the first frost. The blooms are everlasting when dried.

CULTIVATION

Sow seeds directly in the garden after danger of frost, or start seeds indoors 4 to 6 weeks ahead. Seeds require warm soil (75°F) to sprout. Use caution; disturb the roots as little as possible when transplanting, as damaged roots result in slow growth. Thin or plant 18 to 24 inches apart in average garden soil. The plants need little or no fertilizer. Love-lies-bleeding thrives in hot weather and dry soil, but water during drought. Overwatering may cause root rot. Plants may need staking.

COMMENTS: *A. tricolor*, known as Joseph's Coat, is another old-fashioned annual that has spectacularly colored leaves of red, green, and yellow. Both make unusual houseplants.

POSITION: Sun.

PROPAGATION: Seed.

Marigold

African Marigold, *Tagetes erecta*
French Marigold, *Tagetes patula*

FOLKLORE

All marigolds are native to Mexico, yet two of the oldest varieties are named African marigolds and French marigolds. Introduced in a roundabout way, African marigolds (*T. erecta*) were first brought to Spain early in the sixteenth century. The plants became popular in southern Europe under the name of rose of India. *T. erecta* plants made their way to northern Africa, where they naturalized. Many thought them a local flower, and eventually they become known as African marigolds.

The French marigold (*T. patula*) was brought from France to England in 1573, and named to differentiate it from the pot marigold (calendula). Legend states that it first bloomed the year after the Massacre of St. Bartholomew in 1572.

Very popular in the Americas, Native Americans grew marigolds for medicinal purposes. Later, Thomas Jefferson recorded in April of 1810 the planting of African marigolds in his garden. Marigolds remained vastly popular and were the subject of a $10,000 reward, posted by a leading seed company, for the producer of a pure white variety.

The genus was named after Tages, a Roman demi-god celebrated for his beauty. Tages was the grandson of Jupiter and is said to have taught the Etruscans the art of divination.

DESCRIPTION

Masses of golden color are the trademark of marigolds. Blooms come in brilliant hues of orange, yellow, white, burgundy, and bi-color. Flowers are single or double, and grow atop dark green, divided foliage. Contrary to popular belief, the scent is not offensive.

African marigolds, often called Aztec marigolds, grow 10 to 36 inches high— generally taller than French marigolds. Striking plants with flowers similar to large carnations, they come in dwarf, medium, and tall types, making them versatile in the garden.

French marigolds grow 6 to 20 inches high and are bushier and more compact plants than the African marigolds. Flower heads are single or double and somewhat smaller than the African types. The single flowers have a daisy-like appearance.

CULTIVATION

One of the easiest flowers to grow, marigolds need little more care than watering. Sow seeds directly in the ground after danger of frost or start indoors. Because they grow so quickly, it's generally easier to sow in place. African marigolds take longer to bloom than the French, so either start them indoors in late winter or purchase young plants. Space about half the height of the plant. Average, not-too-rich, well-drained soil is best, but these hardy flowers will grow in any soil. Fertilize when planting, but usually not again. Pick faded flowers to prolong bloom time. Marigolds thrive in heat; water during dry spells. Tall plants will need staking. Marigolds are perfect for beginner gardeners, as well as for children.

POSITION: Sun.

PROPAGATION: Seed.

Mixed marigolds (above). *Tagetes erecta* 'Antique Primrose' (opposite).

Morning Glory

Dwarf Morning Glory

Convolvulus tricolor

FOLKLORE

Morning glory is often called life of man. It has served as a symbol of the transience of man's life: its flowers begin opening in the morning (birth), are in full bloom by midday (vigor), and fade in the evening (old age).

Superstition has long maintained that morning glory is used by witches, who are said to pluck the flowers three days before the full moon to make their powers particularly potent. The seeds of the plant are poisonous and are known in some cases to cause hallucinations—which may explain the con-nection between morning glories and witchcraft.

Morning glories were a favorite flower with the seventeenth-century Dutch and Flemish and are often seen in their paintings. In *The Language of Flowers*, it denotes affectation.

The genus name *Convolvulus* is from the Latin *convolvere*, meaning "to bind or cling." It aptly de-scribes other members of the same family that bind themselves to other plants and are invasive, among them, field bindweed.

DESCRIPTION

A charming, old-fashioned garden plant, dwarf morning glories nevertheless have fallen out of favor since our grandmothers' time. These cheerful blue-purple flowers with yellow throats encircled by a white ring bloom profusely all summer long. Flowers are funnel-shaped, about 1½ inches across. Their dark-green foliage forms a mounded clump. Unlike its vining relatives, these dwarf morning glories reach only 12 inches high and their flowers remain open all day. An annual, they are excellent for bedding and are quite nice in hanging baskets.

CULTIVATION

Sow seeds directly in place after final frost. Seeds may be started indoors, but transplanting is somewhat difficult; plant in peat pots to minimize root disturbance. Start 4 to 6 weeks before putting out. To speed germination, nick the hard seed coat with a knife or soak seeds in water overnight before planting. Average, well-drained soil is sufficient. For maximum flowering, avoid rich soil and do not fertilize. Space plants 12 to 15 inches apart to give them plenty of room to spread. Full sun and not too much water are their sole requirements.

COMMENTS: The morning glory vine (*Ipomoea*) is a climber with similar, but much larger, flowers than the dwarf morning glory.

POSITION: Sun.

PROPAGATION: Seed, division, or cuttings.

Nasturtium

Indian Cress

Tropaeolum majus

FOLKLORE

Native to Peru and the West Indies, nasturtiums were first sent to Spain in the late 1500s. By 1680, the flower was so well known in Europe that few gardens were without it. Doubles were cultivated in the 1700s. The semi-double type was grown from a plant found in California; in 1931, it received the American Award of Merit, and by the next year was so popular that literally tons of seeds were insufficient to supply the demand.

Nasturtium gained its common name, Indian cress, from the hot, peppery taste of its leaves, which is not unlike the flavor of watercress, *Nasturtium officinale*. Nasturtiums have long been used for flavoring and in folk remedies. Old recipe books list nasturtium as an ingredient in salads, garnishes, and mustards. The seeds and flowers were eaten by sailors at sea to combat scurvy.

The Swedish botanist Carolus Linnaeus named the genus with the Latin word *tropaeum*, "trophy," because the round leaf suggests a shield, and the flower, a helmet stained with blood.

DESCRIPTION

Bright, gay nasturtiums have graced gardens for centuries. Flowers bloom profusely all summer long on compact, bushy or semi-trailing varieties. The compact, bushy varieties grow to 12 inches high and are often referred to as dwarfs. The semi-trailing kind grow to 24 inches high, but can trail up to 12 feet. Flowers come in single, semidouble, or double cup-shaped, in red, yellow, orange, pink, white, and some bi-colors. Some are fragrant. The foliage is light green and rounded or lobed. Both the leaves and flowers are edible. The leaves have a peppery taste, desirable in salads. Trailing nasturtiums are beautiful hanging from window boxes. Due to their extensive trails, they are particularly stunning from second story windows. These annuals are also excellent for containers and baskets.

CULTIVATION

Nasturtiums need little care; they often thrive in the poorest of soils. Sow outdoors in place after danger of frost. Seeds may be started indoors, but seedlings do not transplant well. Ideal soil is light and not too rich; too much fertilizer produces more leaves and fewer flowers. Space 8 to 12 inches apart and do not overwater; water only when soil is dry. Nasturtiums flower best in cool and humid conditions. They grow rapidly and are extremely sensitive to frost.

COMMENTS: Easy to grow, nasturtiums make good plants for children's gardens. The bush-type nasturtiums do better in warmer climates.

POSITION: Sun or part shade.

Mixed nasturtium (above). 'Strawberries and Cream' (opposite).

Peony

Paeonia, *lactiflora* hybrids

FOLKLORE

Peonies are often called the oldest of all plants. Described in Theophrastus's *Enquiry into Plants* in 320 B.C., the wild European flower was named for Paean, a physician to the Greek gods, and known as the god of healing, who used its roots to cure Pluto from a wound inflicted by Hercules.

Native to China and Japan, the peony grown in our gardens was described during the Tang dynasty (ca. 600) in song and poetry, and its image was used to decorate imperial palaces. Tree peonies became so treasured during this time that choice varieties were sold for a hundred ounces of gold and more.

Valued not just for their beauty, peonies have also been prized for practical purposes. Seeds were used for flavoring and as a condiment in foods. They were also taken with wine or mead to ward off nightmares. Peony roots were used to treat epilepsy. Peonies, too, were thought to drive away evil spirits, prevent storms—and so were used as charms against witchcraft.

Peonies came to America with European settlers. By 1876, the peony was chosen to represent the spirit, ambition, and determination of America at the Philadelphia Centennial Exposition.

DESCRIPTION

Spectacular and fragrant, peonies are favorites of everyone. Beautiful, large flowers bloom 3 to 6 inches across in pink, red, white, salmon, and creamy yellow. Their deep, glossy-green foliage emerges from a group of reddish shoots and form a neat clump 2 to 3 feet high. Flowers bloom on long stems, making them ideal for cutting. There are five basic peony flower forms: double, semidouble, Japanese, anemone, and singles. All are beautiful. Flowers bloom in May and June, but, by choosing a selection of early-, mid-, and late-blooming kinds, peonies can bloom successively for up to six weeks.

CULTIVATION

Peonies require minimum care. Purchase plants from a reliable grower and plant two inches below ground level in deep, rich soil, amended with lots of organic matter. Space 2 to 3 feet apart. Water adequately, especially during dry spells. Fertilize each spring with well-rotted manure or slow-release fertilizer. For larger flowers, leave only the central bud on each stalk. Young or newly-planted peonies may not bloom the first year or so until they become established. Once established, they are incredibly long-lived and can be left undisturbed for generation after generation.

Peonies do not perform as well in subtropical areas, such as the Southwest or Southeast.

COMMENTS: Tree peonies are shrubs, not trees, that grow 3 to 4 feet. They have larger flowers than the herbaceous plants described here, but are not as easily grown.

POSITION: Sun or part shade.

PROPAGATION: Division.

Paeonia 'Globe of Light' (above). *Paeonia* 'Festiva Maxima' (opposite).

Phlox

Garden Phlox
Phlox paniculata

FOLKLORE

All phloxes, except one, are indigenous to North America. Garden phlox first arrived in Europe in 1752, and became very popular in England during the 1800s. Even though a native flower, Americans did not grow it much until it was re-exported from Europe to America in the late 1800s.

In Victorian England, phlox was gathered into bouquets and sent to loved ones as a wish for pleas-ant dreams. Phlox might even imply a proposal of marriage. In *The Language of Flowers*, it was made a symbol of unanimity.

The Greek name *phlox* means "flame," and was used by Theophrastus for some unidentified flower with a fiery bloom. The Roman Pliny has told how the Greeks wove phlox garlands, but this is certainly not the plant we now call phlox, as it was not yet in-troduced to the Old World.

DESCRIPTION

Known as garden phlox, border phlox, or summer phlox—by any name, it has been a staple in gardens for generations. Masses of five-petaled flowers are clustered together to form large heads 10 to 12 inches across that bloom in July to early September. Tall stalks rise 3 to 4 feet above dense foliage with blooms in pink, magenta, purple, lavender, blue, or white. Garden phloxes are particularly cherished for their sweet scent, which is noticeably strongest at dusk. White and pale-colored varieties are often planted in white or evening gardens for their luminosity as well as for their fragrance.

CULTIVATION

Phlox is easy to grow, but requires some maintenance for best appearance. Plant in moist, well-drained soil rich in organic matter. Water frequently at ground level, but be careful not to dampen the leaves; too much dampness causes mildew and fungus on the leaves and stems. Space 18 to 24 inches apart for good air circulation to prevent these diseases. Fertilize regularly. Remove spent blooms for more flowers and to keep plants from self-sowing. Cultivars revert back to magenta parents. Phlox may require staking. Divide every 3 to 4 years. This perennial is easier to grow from purchased plants than to start from seed.

COMMENTS: Other types of phlox are: *P. divaricata*, blue phlox, which grows 12 to 15 inches and blooms in the spring; *P. bifida*, prairie phlox, which grows to 10 inches and blooms in the spring; and *P. subulata*, moss pink, which grows 6 inches high and blooms in the spring.

POSITION: Sun or part shade.

PROPAGATION: Seed, division, or cuttings.

Pincushion Flower

Scabiosa atropurpurea, S. caucasia

FOLKLORE

Cultivated in gardens since 1629, pincushion flower received its common name from the English; the silvery stamens in the center of the blooms protrude above the flower head like pins stuck in a pincushion. Because of its original deep-purple shade, other popular names for the flower are widow-in-mourning and mourning bride. The deep purple-black color of pincushion flowers inspired their use as memorial flowers throughout the Mediterannean, where the flower is native.

The annual *S. atropurpurea* was introduced in 1629 from the Mediterranean. The perennial form, *S. caucasia*, reached England from Mt. Caucasus at the beginning of the nineteenth century; soon after, it became one of the most popular cut flowers in the British Isles. Pincushion flowers came to the United States from England and became colonial favorites.

In *The Language of Flowers*, pincushion flowers symbolize unfortunate love or widowhood.

DESCRIPTION

Once quite fashionable, this old-fashioned favorite is making a comeback in both its perennial and annual forms. Annual pincushion flowers are somewhat larger, bloom slightly longer, and are much more fragrant than the perennial. The annuals have richly colored flowers in blue, dark purple, deep maroon, rose, and white on long stems that grow 18 to 36 inches high, and bloom continuously from midsummer to October. These tall plants bear dozens of deliciously fragrant flowers on each stem.

The perennial grows 12 to 24 inches high and comes mostly in pastel blues, but white and pink are also available. The scent is faint and subtle, and flowers bloom from July to September. Both forms have the characteristic fat centers that resemble a cushion stuck full of pins. Flowers are 2 to 3 inches across and are host to bees and butterflies all summer, especially the monarch, fritillary, and skipper butterflies. Pincushion flower makes an excellent long-lasting cut flower.

CULTIVATION

Very easy to grow from seed, pincushion flowers can be started indoors 4 to 6 weeks before the last frost. They may also be sown in place after danger of frost. Perennials sometimes bloom the first year. Pincushion flowers are easily cultivated in ordinary soil, but will thrive in rich, well-drained soil. Space 10 to 12 inches apart. Water moderately, mostly in dry spells and water in the morning to prevent mildew. Fertilize when planting. Although quite hardy, these flowers perform less well in extreme heat and in soggy conditions. Remove faded blooms to prolong flowering. Divide perennials every 3 to 4 years.

POSITION: Sun or light shade.
PROPAGATION: Seed or division.

Poppy

Field Poppy, Flanders Poppy, Corn Poppy
Papaver species

FOLKLORE

In classical mythology, the poppy, with its abundance of seeds, was the symbol of life and fertility for Cybele, the earth goddess. The Opium poppy (*P. somniferum*) is the oldest species in cultivation and, according to the Greeks and Romans, was created by Somnus, the god of sleep. Because of its narcotic qualities, it is also known as the flower of sleep. Its seeds were found on prehistoric sites, used by Egyptians in burial rites, and Greek athletes used them for training for the Olympics. It is this plant that is usually represented in Dutch flower paintings. The common field poppy (*P. rhoeas*) is the one painted by the Impressionists, and its beauty captivated many in the Art Nouveau movement.

The poppy is also the symbol of death, immortalized in John McCrae's poem about World War I, "In Flanders Fields," which describes how field poppies now grow by the thousands where where thousands of soldiers once lay dead.

Common in colonial gardens, Thomas Jefferson grew both the field poppy and the large, white opium poppy at Monticello.

DESCRIPTION

Poppies are one of the most beautiful of flowers, equally at home in the country or in a formal garden. Poppies are available in annual, biennial, and perennial forms. All look similar. The annual field poppy (*P. rhoeas*) has numerous common names, including the Flanders poppy and the corn poppy. It is also known as the Shirley poppy because of the hybrids developed by the English breeder of the same name. The field poppy grows 1 to 2 feet, comes in a variety of colors, and blooms in early summer, from late May through June. The Iceland poppy (*P. nudicaule*), a biennial, comes in pastel colors and darker shades, with flowers up to 4 or 5 inches across in semidoubles and doubles. It is somewhat more difficult to grow than the field poppy. The Oriental poppy (*P. orientale*) has flowers up to 8 inches across, most commonly in red with large black centers. This easy and very hardy perennial blooms in early summer.

CULTIVATION

Most poppies do not transplant well, so sow seeds directly where you want them, either in late fall or early spring as soon as the soil can be worked. Poppies need darkness for germination, but barely cover the seeds and keep them moist. Well-drained soil is essential, and soil rich in organic matter is ideal. Space 10 to 12 inches apart and fertilize only when planting. Water only as needed; be careful not to overwater. Annual poppies do best in regions with cool summers. In warmer areas, the Orientals will do best if given some shade. If the ground is not disturbed, many of the annual poppies will self-sow. The field poppy has a short life; its foliage dies down and disappears after flowering, so plant it where other flowers can take its place. The Oriental poppy can be purchased from nurseries, rather than grown from seed, and, once established, is long-lived.

COMMENTS: The flower commonly called the California poppy (*Eschscholzia californica*), although in the poppy family, belongs to another genus. See Poppy, California.

POSITION: Sun.

Field poppies (above). Oriental poppies (opposite).

Poppy, California

Eschscholzia californica

FOLKLORE

Native to California and Oregon, the California poppy grows wild and naturalizes freely in fields, prairies, along the coast, and in semi-desert regions. At one time, intensely orange California poppies were so abundant along the coast that the Spaniards called the country The Land of Fire and The Golden West; the common Spanish name given the flowers translates to cup of gold. In 1826, the California poppy was introduced in England. By 1833 its golden brilliance was common sight in cottage gardens. Like other poppies, the California poppy has been used by herbalists and by Native Americans for its narcotic properties, particularly soothing for headaches.

The California poppy is a member of the poppy family, but belongs to a different genus, *Eschscholzia*, named for Johann Friedrich Eschscholz (1793-1835). Eschscholz, a German doctor and naturalist, was a member of an expedition that sailed to the Pacific coast of North America in 1815.

The California poppy is the state flower of California.

DESCRIPTION

The California poppy has brilliant, cup-shaped, orange-yellow flowers on 12 to 18 inch stems. The flowers are 2 to 3 inches across and consist of 4 delicate petals. The golden color is the original, but many hybrids are now available in shades of yellow, orange, scarlet, cream, copper, and rosy-red. The silvery-green foliage is deeply divided. Flowers remain closed during wet or cloudy weather. Individual flowers are short-lived, but new buds are produced in abundance throughout the summer, so plants provide a continous display of flowers from early summer to frost. California poppies are most effective when grown in large groups.

CULTIVATION

Beautiful and hardy, California poppies need a minimum of soil and a maximum of sun, and they will grow almost anywhere. The ideal soil should be warm and rather dry and sandy. Sow seed as early as possible in spring where the plants are to grow. Seeds may also be sown in September or October; plants will bloom earlier the next spring from this autumn sowing. Keep soil moist for germination. Thin to 6 inches apart. California poppies thrive in hot weather; water only during droughts. Remove faded blooms to prolong flowering. These poppies naturalize freely by self-sown seed, but hybrids will revert back to golden parent.

POSITION: Sun.

PROPAGATION: Seed.

Primrose

English Primrose
Primula vulgaris (syn. *P. acaulis*)

FOLKLORE

One of the best-known of all flowers and one of the most popular plants throughout history, the primrose has been for centuries especially beloved of the English. It is mentioned by Chaucer in *The Miller's Tale,* referred to by Shakespeare in several plays, and described in poetry by many, including Keats, Coleridge, Milton, and Spenser. Queen Victoria sent Prime Minister Benjamin Disraeli primroses every year on his birthday and honored him with a large wreath of "his favorite flower" at his funeral.

Primroses are found growing wild in fields, in ditches, and along hedgerows in England and southern Europe. They were grown enthusiastically in Tudor gardens, where they graced manor houses and cottages alike. Early settlers in North America brought primrose seed from Europe; the flowers were grown in the colonial gardens at Williamsburg, Virginia. They were also grown at Monticello, Mount Vernon, and Andrew Jackson's Hermitage.

The name primrose is from the Latin *primus,* meaning "first," and refers to the early-blooming habit of these flowers.

DESCRIPTION

English primroses are hardy perennials that naturalize easily throughout the garden. Among the most colorful and easy-to-grow garden plants, primroses come in pale yellow, salmon, red, rose, purple, and white, some with contrasting eyes, and some with double flowers. They grow 5 to 10 inches high and have a light, delicate scent. The leaves form a clump at the base of the plant and the foliage is a wrinkled, deep green. Short, leafless stalks of flowers emerge, giving each plant the look of a small bouquet. Primroses bloom for two months in April and May, and often reappear in fall or early winter. In warm climates, they remain evergreen.

CULTIVATION

English primroses are easy to start from nursery plants or to sow from seed in late winter or early spring. Germination requires light, so do not cover the seeds and keep them moist. Soil should be a rich, moist loam, well-drained, with lots of organic matter added. Space plants 6 inches apart. Plants like cool, moist areas, so water regularly and keep mulched. They do nicely near water, but not in it, and will not survive a summer drought. Primroses can be successfully transplanted in full bloom; even if you purchase one impulsively at the grocery store, it can be planted and will rebloom for years. Primroses self-sow in favorable conditions and are very long-lived plants. Divide after blooming for best results.

COMMENTS: Polyanthus primroses (*Primula* x *polyanthes*) are not quite as celebrated as the English primroses, but are just as old-fashioned and easy to grow. They are available in all colors but blue and red. A variety of other primroses are available, but are too extensive to describe here. Some are rather difficult to grow.

POSITION: Shade.

PROPAGATION: Seed or division.

English primrose (right and left). Polyanthus primrose (opposite).

Snapdragon

Antirrhinum majus

FOLKLORE

The snapdragon takes its name from its flowers that resemble the head and jaws of a dragon. If the throat is pinched, the "jaws" open. Among its other common names are lion's snap, toad's mouth, and dog's mouth. Another moniker, calf's snout, is inspired by the shape and black color of the snapdragon's seed pods.

In ancient lore, the snapdragon possesses supernatural powers. If the flower is hung around the neck, it provides protection from witchcraft. Its magical powers are also said to restore beauty and youthfulness to women who wash their faces with the water rendered from the seeds. A woman who washes in snapdragon water and wears the leaves in her shoe makes herself nearly irresistible.

Snapdragons are native to southern Europe. It was probably the original purple-flowering species which Thomas Jefferson grew in Virginia and found suitable for naturalizing in 1771. Also native to the Mediterranean, snapdragons were grown for the oil made from their seed, which was used in cooking as a substitute for olive oil.

DESCRIPTION

One of the most charming and colorful flowers in the garden, snapdragons are available in dwarf, medium, and tall varieties. Among the most versatile bed and border plants, they come in shades of white, pink, red, yellow, apricot, and purple. Stately, erect spires of blooms cover dark, dense foliage. Snapdragons grows 10 to 36 inches high, depending on the type, and bloom heavily in early summer. If faded blooms are cut, snapdragons will bloom again in fall. Some varieties are faintly scented. Snapdragons make beautiful, long-lasting cut flowers.

CULTIVATION

For earliest blooms, start indoors 8 to 12 weeks before the last frost or buy young seedlings. Seeds may be sown outdoors in spring in warm soil. Do not cover the seeds; light is needed for germination. Space 6 to 8 inches apart. When seedlings are about 3 inches tall, pinch out the center stem so the plant will bush out. Fertilize when planting and again monthly. Soil should be moderately rich, well-drained, and rather high in lime content, but plants will endure a wide range of soils. Snapdragons tolerate heat and light frosts. Remove spent blooms for more flowering—if seed heads are not removed, the plant will die out. To eliminate additional maintenance, plant rust-resistant cultivars. Taller cultivars will need staking. Snapdragons self-sow freely; they show up in the oddest places, even in old walls.

POSITION: Sun or light shade.
PROPAGATION: Seed or cuttings.

Spiderwort

Tradescantia virginiana

FOLKLORE

Native to North America from Maine to South Dakota and Arkansas, spiderwort was introduced in England in the seventeenth century. The silky foliage and exceptional blooms were soon fancied by many English gardeners. By 1650, spiderwort was to be found in virtually every cottager's garden in England.

It is commonly thought that the English gave spiderwort its name. Early botanists classified spiderwort as one of the Phalangiums, which were believed to cure the bite of the poisonous Phalangium spider (now known to be harmless). The plant was renamed in 1718. But spiderwort might also take its name from its long, drooping leaves that look like a spider suspended on a trail of web filament. Other common names include Trinity flower because of its three petals, and widow's tears because spiderwort flowers do not dry up upon flowering, but turn into a wet blot.

Spiderwort takes its botanical name from John Tradescant the Elder, the royal gardener to King Charles I of England. Plants were first sent to England by Tradescant from Virginia. Tradescant, on a plant expedition to America, first thought spiderwort was a silky grass.

92

DESCRIPTION

Spiderworts have attractive, three-petaled flowers on 2- to 3-foot stems. Flowers traditionally come in blue-violet, but white, pink, and rosy-red varieties are also available. Colorful clusters of blooms provide flowers over a long season, from June to August. Each flower lasts for only one day, but bloom is continuous due to the multitude of flowers. Straplike, deep-green leaves are 1 inch wide and extend from the plant's base in clumps. Divide this perennial in spring or fall.

CULTIVATION

Extremely easy to grow, spiderworts adapt to many difficult situations, including poor soil, deep shade, soggy ground, and other wet conditions. They even thrive on neglect in abandoned areas. Start seed in early spring or sow newly harvested seed in late fall for bloom the next year. Grow in part shade in almost any kind of soil. Plants perform best if kept moist. Cut back untidy foliage after flowering and leaves will re-emerge; sometimes plants will bloom again. Spiderworts are vigorous plants that have a tendency to sprawl; divide plants every 2 to 3 years and keep fertilizer to a minimum to prevent them from running.

COMMENTS: Spiderworts are well suited to the border or, planted in clumps, in the wild garden. Use *T.* x *adersoniana* and *T. ohiensis* for boggy spots; *T. hirsuticaulis* will tolerate drier soils.

POSITION: Part shade or sun.

PROPAGATION: Seed, division, or cuttings.

Spiderwort 'Red Cloud' (above). Common spiderwort (opposite).

Sunflower

Helianthus annuus

FOLKLORE

Sunflowers are featured in many myths of Native Americans of the Southwest. In Hopi lore, when sunflowers are plentiful, the harvest will be good. Many tribes mention Sunflowers in songs and rituals, including a Zuni rainmaker dance. The sunflower is also used extensively as a motif in Native American art and decoration, and is used in cooking, dyes, and paint making, and as a hair tonic.

In Peru, the sunflower was held in great honor as the emblem of the Inca Sun God. The flowers were carved into ancient Inca temples and medallions of gold molded into sunflowers were worn by their priests and priestesses.

In 1805, explorers Lewis and Clark noted an abundance of sunflowers growing wild. When the first party of Mormons travelled from Missouri, they scattered sunflower seeds across the plains to mark the route in sunflower trails for the next wave of settlers. Pioneers of the West used them for food and sunflower oil was used, then as now, in cooking.

DESCRIPTION

The cheery, common sunflower grows from 4 to 12 feet high. Large flower heads come in traditional bright yellows and golds, and newer varieties are orange, brown, and white. Blooms spread as much as 1 foot across, and all have dark centers.

Bloom time is July to September. Sunflowers attract many kinds of birds, who visit the plants to eat the seeds. Sunflowers are excellent plants for children's gardens and for beginning gardeners.

CULTIVATION

Extremely heat and drought tolerant, sunflowers will grow in almost any conditions. Sow seeds outdoors where you want them to grow, after the last frost. Starting seeds indoors is not necessary; the plants grow so quickly. Sunflowers are best planted 2 to 4 feet apart in light, well-drained, dry soil—but practically any soil will do. Fertilize sparingly, if at all. Do not overwater; the plants are very tolerant of heat and drought. The taller varieties require staking.

COMMENTS: *H. annuus* grows 4 to 5 feet, *H. giganteus* grows 9 to 12 feet. Many other varieties now on the market offer diversity in height and color. There are shorter, bushier plants (only 15 inches high) and even a white sunflower!

POSITION: Sun.

PROPAGATION: Seed.

Tobacco, Flowering

Jasmine Tobacco

Nicotiana alata, N. sylvestris

FOLKLORE

In 1492, Christopher Columbus's crew witnessed natives of Hispaniola smoking dried leaves. These were the leaves of *Nicotiana tabacum*, known in English as tobacco. In 1560, Jean Nicot, the French Ambassador to Portugal, planted it in his garden in Lisbon for its dried leaves, which were used as snuff. He later sent seeds to Catherine de Médici at the French court. In 1586, Sir Francis Drake imported it into England from Virginia. He introduced tobacco smoking to the English court and, thus, tobacco became an important cash crop in America.

Native to South America, the plant was called "tobacco" because it had first been introduced from Tobago in the West Indies. The popular flowering tobacco (*N. alata*), a tender perennial, was introduced from Brazil in 1829 and became immediately successful in gardens because of its delicious fragrance and its ease of culture. Flowering tobacco is also native to Uruguay, Paraguay, and Argentina.

The genus name *Nicotiana* is after Jean Nicot, who not only introduced flowering tobacco to the French court, but also grew it in his garden.

DESCRIPTION

Irresistible, old-fashioned annuals grown for their intoxicating fragrance, flowering tobaccos have been popular for generations. N. alata grows 3 to 4 feet in height and bears star-shaped, white flowers that bloom from June until September. Flowers open at dusk and emit a deeply scented perfume that is perceptible several yards away. A bouquet will infuse an entire room with fragrance.

N. sylvestris is a much larger, more dramatic plant than N. alata, sometimes growing to 5 or 6 feet. Its oblong, pure green leaves form a basal rosette 1 to 2 feet wide, from which the stems appear. The foliage is quite showy and provides a bold contrast to other plants. The white flowers are long and tubular, and bloom from late July into fall. N. sylvestris is also fragrant, but less so than N. alata. Plant either or both near the porch or deck to enjoy the fragrance fully. The white flowers are illuminated on moonlit evenings, and attract unusual and beautiful nocturnal moths.

CULTIVATION

Extremely easy to grow from seed, sow flowering tobacco inside 6 to 8 weeks before the last frost, or scatter the seed in the garden just after the last frost. Light aids germination, so press seeds lightly into the soil, but do not cover. Set out in the garden 12 to 18 inches apart in any ordinary garden soil. Pinch back the leaves for bushier plants. Water only during dry spells and apply a balanced fertilizer once a month. Deadheading is not neccessary, although it may encourage plants to bloom a little longer. In warm climates, they will often become perennial. It is rarely neccessary to sow seed again, as nicotianas are abundant self-sowers.

COMMENTS: Nicotiana hybrids such as the Domino or Nikki series, are small, compact plants that bloom during the day and are not fragrant.

POSITION: Part shade or sun.

PROPAGATION: Seed.

Nicotiana alata (above). Nicotiana sylvestris (opposite).

Verbena

Verbena x hybrida

FOLKLORE

The Roman gods considered verbena to be a sacred herb. It was placed on the altar of Jupiter, and throughout the Roman Empire, messages of peace were sent with crowns of verbena. The Romans thought verbena possessed the power to rekindle the flames of dying love; they named it *herba veneris*, or plant of Venus, the goddess of love.

Celtic druids also cherished verbena and used it in rituals. During the Middle Ages and the Renaissance, it was used to ward off witches and sorcerers. Verbena was also used to treat rheumatic pains, pleurisy, lumbago, and the bites of rabid dogs. It was even used as an aphrodisiac; brides wore verbena in their hair for good luck.

Verbena hybrids were introduced from South America between 1826 and 1837. Their vivid coloring made them an immensely popular bedding plant, promoting competition and exhibition of the new varieties. By the 1880s, there were nearly 100 named varieties.

DESCRIPTION

A rich carpet of brilliantly colored verbena blooming is a sight to behold. Its continuous bloom from June to frost makes it perfect for the front of the border or to brighten a hot, dry spot. Verbena's small, tubular flowers emerge in dense clusters 3 to 4 inches across, and come in blooms of white, pink, red, lavender, blue, and purple, some with white eyes. The leaves are toothed, textured, and thick. Plants are low and trailing, spreading along the ground and rooting as they go. Height can vary between 8 to 18 inches, depending on variety. Verbena is excellent as an edging plant or in window boxes and containers. Verbena also make fine cut flowers. At one time verbena was extremely fragrant, but the scent has been lost through hybridization.

CULTIVATION

Buy verbena as young plants, as they are somewhat difficult to start from seed. This will also allow you to select the colors you want—plants from seed may not all come true to specified colors. They do just fine in average soil, but perform better in sandy, well-drained, rich soil. Verbena is quite tolerant of heat, but needs good air circulation, so place plants 12 to 18 inches apart. Water only moderately; verbena is prone to mildew in damp locations. Fertilize regularly. To start seeds, begin indoors 10 to 12 weeks before setting out. Refrigerate seeds for a week before sowing. Seeds need darkness to germinate, but do not cover. Seeds are highly prone to damping off disease, so water sparingly. Seeds may be sown out-of-doors in May for late summer bloom, and if covered with a loose mulch of branches and leaves, it may winter over. Plants may be brought indoors and wintered over; take cuttings

POSITION: Sun.

PROPAGATION: Seed, division, or cuttings.

Mixed verbena hybrids (above). *Verbena* 'Imagination' (opposite).

Violet

Violets, Pansies, Johnny-Jump-Ups
Viola cornuta, V. tricolor,
V. odorata, V. x wittrockiana

FOLKLORE

In Greek mythology, Zeus took a fancy to Io, daughter of the river god Inachus. But Hera, Zeus's wife, caught wind of the dalliance, so Zeus transformed Io into a heifer to protect her from the jealous wrath of his spouse. Mere grass was not good enough for this special bovine, so Zeus created violets for his Io-turned-heifer to graze upon.

Violets and pansies are described in history, art, and literature through the ages. In the *Odyssey*, Homer writes of the sweet-smelling violets that grow on the island of Calypso. The violet was the emblematic flower of ancient Athens, and many Greeks are immortalized in statues crowned with violet wreathes. The Romans used them to adorn their banquet tables. The French became manic about them in the 1700s; violets became the emblem of the Bonapartists, since Napoleon had promised to return from Elba when the violets were in bloom. And in Italy, the city of Parma adopted the violet as its symbol and began the manufacture of its famous Parma violet perfume.

DESCRIPTION

Favorites of everyone, violets have rich, velvety blooms that come in purple, lavender, white, and yellow. Pansies come in brilliant colors of almost every hue, some bi-color. These low-growing plants are 4 to 12 inches tall. A true delight of late winter and early spring, they are able to withstand light frosts. Violets bloom in the spring and early summer. Pansies bloom in the spring, and, if watered well, some will bloom all summer.

CULTIVATION

Violets and pansies thrive in the shade in cool, humus-rich soil, as well as in alkaline soil. Keep plants watered and fertilize regularly. Highly cold-resistant, violets and pansies may be purchased in packs or flats in early spring. Transplant in rich, well-drained soil, and enjoy blooms until the summer heat wilts them. Sow seed in late July or early August for flowering in early spring. Sow seed in spring for summer use in cool climates. Shade until seedlings appear (darkness is needed for germination). Seeds can also be started 6 to 8 weeks prior to setting out in early spring. Refrigerate seeds for one week before sowing. After seedlings appear and are large enough to handle, transplant to 6-8 inches apart. Keep area weeded and watered. Protect in winter with straw or light mulching material. Remove dead blooms to prolong flowering.

COMMENTS: There are two groups of violets. True violets include *V. cornuta*, tufted violet, and *V. odorata*, sweet violet, the queen of the fragrant violets. These are treated as perennials. The second group are pansies, *V. tricolor,* and many hybrid species known as *V.* x *wittrockiana*, and are usually treated as annuals. Many pansies now come in heat-resistant varieties.

POSITION: Shade or part shade. Some species, like *V.* x *wittrockiana*, do fine in full sun.

PROPAGATION: Seed, division, or cuttings.

Viola 'Princess Blue' (above). *Viola* x *wittrockiana* (opposite).

Zinnia

Youth and Old Age

Zinnia elegans

FOLKLORE

The gardens of Montezuma were a horticultural wonder to the Spanish invaders in the 1520s. Among the flowers in the highly developed Aztec gardens were the zinnia, dahlia, sunflower, and morning glory.

Zinnias were originally considered a Mexican weed. Around the turn of the twentieth century, American hybridists saw the possibilities of zinnias and made many improvements in their blooms. Their success was immediate. Zinnias became very popular, blooming in every border and backyard.

Their popularity in America continues even today.

Zinnias first arrived in Europe around 1750 and were named by Swedish botanist Carolus Linnaeus in honor of Johann Gottfried Zinn (1727-1759), his disciple and professor of botany of the University of Göttingen. The old-fashioned variety was named *elegans*, "elegant." During the Victorian times, zinnias symbolized simplicity. In *The Language of Flowers*, it connotes the thoughts of absent friends.

DESCRIPTION

Zinnias come in an astonishing array of shapes, sizes, forms, and heights, making them very versatile garden plants. Colors range in every variation except blue, and come in single or double blooms. These abundantly blooming annuals last from early summer to frost. Ideal for cutting, the dahlia-like flowers bloom on stems of up to 2 to 3 feet high and are frequented by a multitude of butterflies. The *Zinnia elegans* hybrids have a number of types or classes, such as double (flowers 3 to 4 inches wide), Lilliput or pompon (1 ½ to 2 inches wide), dahlia-flowered (4 to 6 inches wide), Californian giant (6 inches or more in diameter), cactus-flowered (up to 4 inches wide), and Pumila (2 to 3 inches wide).

CULTIVATION

Zinnias need an abundance of hot sun in a warm, moderately dry location. Although not particular about soil, they will thrive in rich, deep soil, either acid or alkaline. Sow seeds directly in the garden after danger of frost. Germination is very rapid, often within 24 hours. Seeds can be started indoors in peat pots to minimize root disturbance. Seedlings can be transplanted when only a few inches high. In the large-flowering types, plants should be topped or pinched when there are three pairs of leaves. This will encourage branching for bushier plants. Snip off old blooms to encourage new growth. Keep the foliage dry to avoid mildew.

COMMENTS: Zinnias are excellent flowers for cutting. Choose buds that are just beginning to open and cut them early in the morning before the heat of the day. They are excellent flowers for beginner gardeners and for children.

POSITION: Sun.

PROPAGATION: Seed.

INDEX OF BOTANICAL NAMES